# Kawaii

## Sweet Treats

# THIS BOOK BELONGS TO

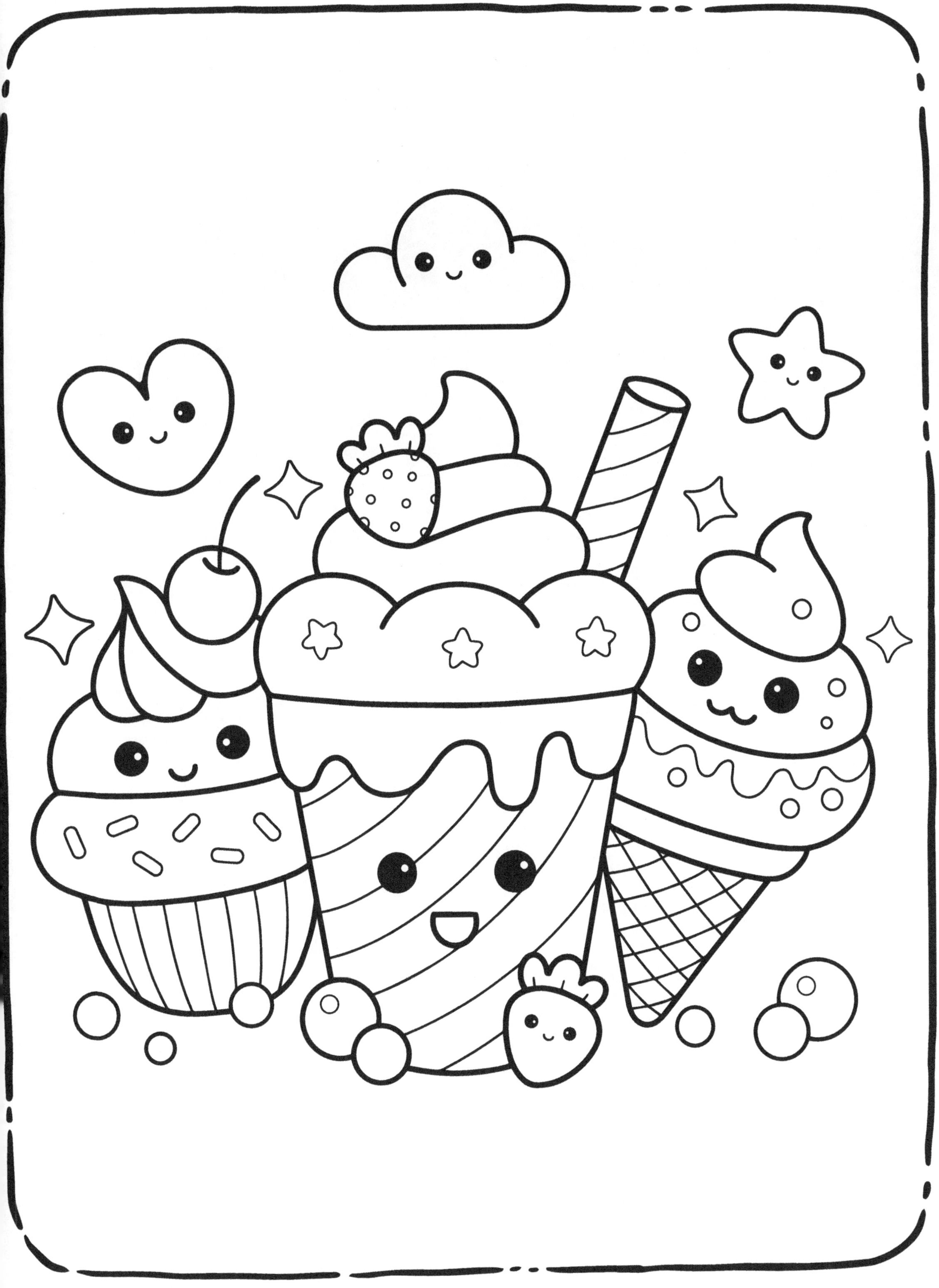

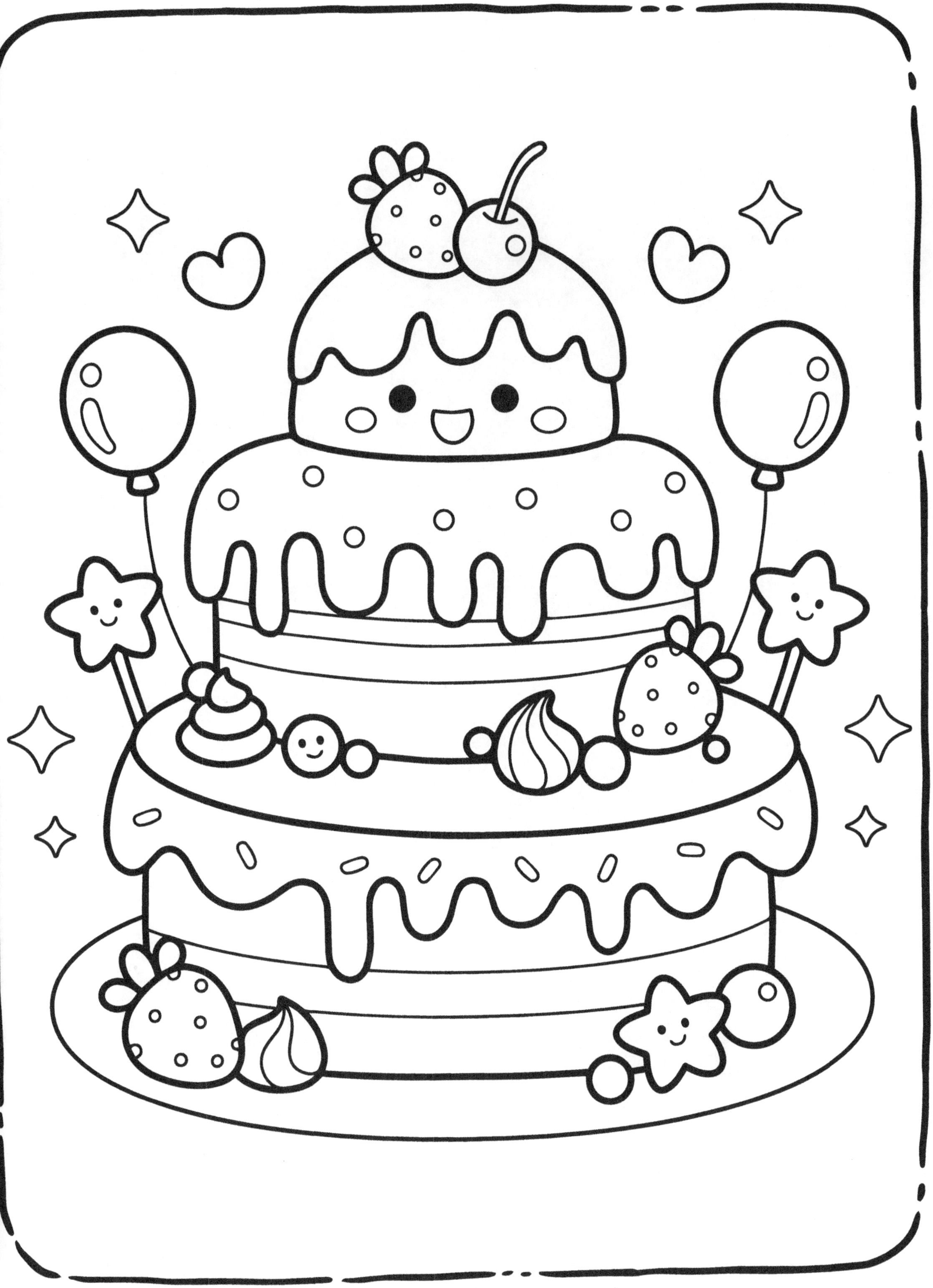

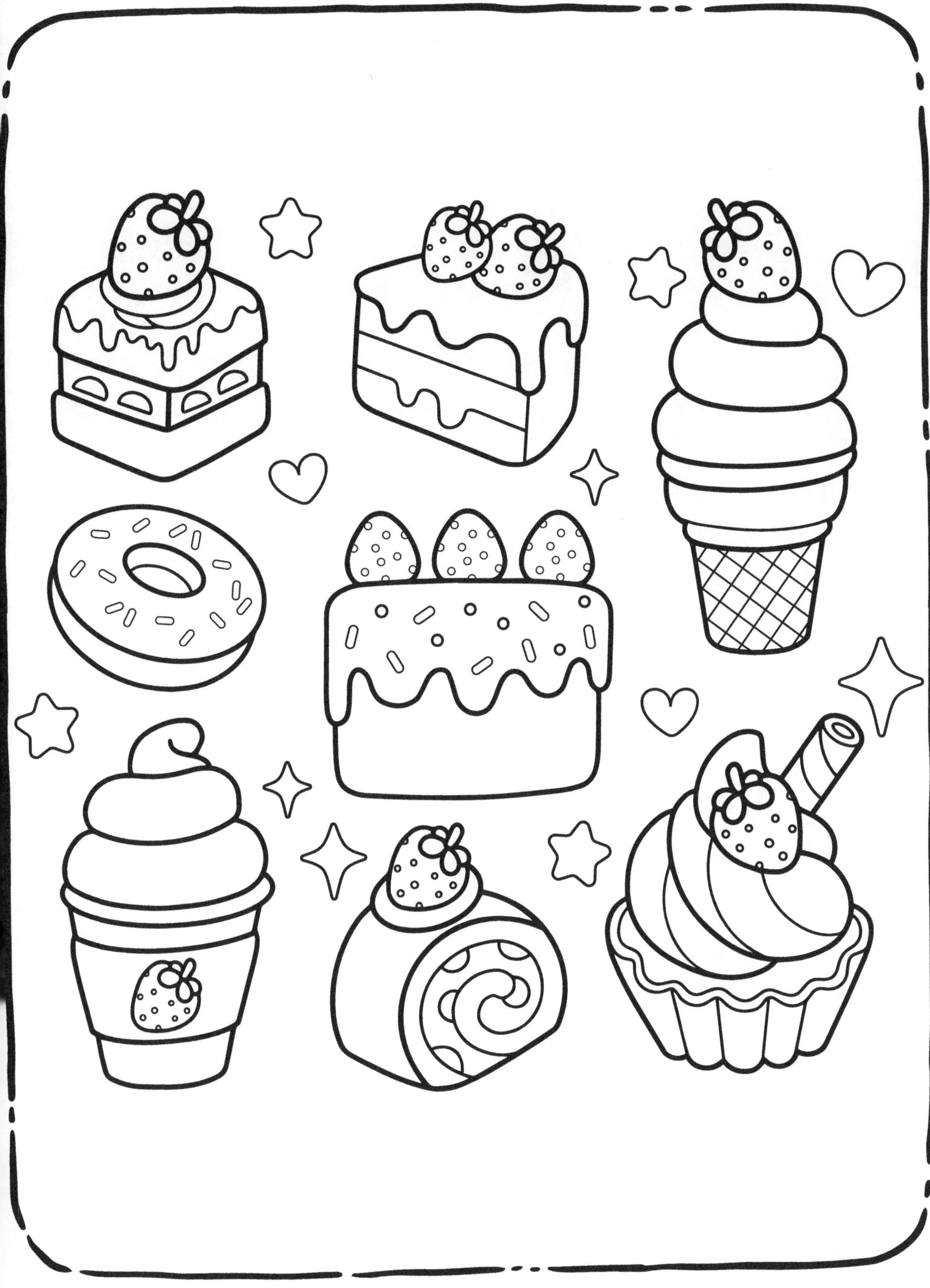

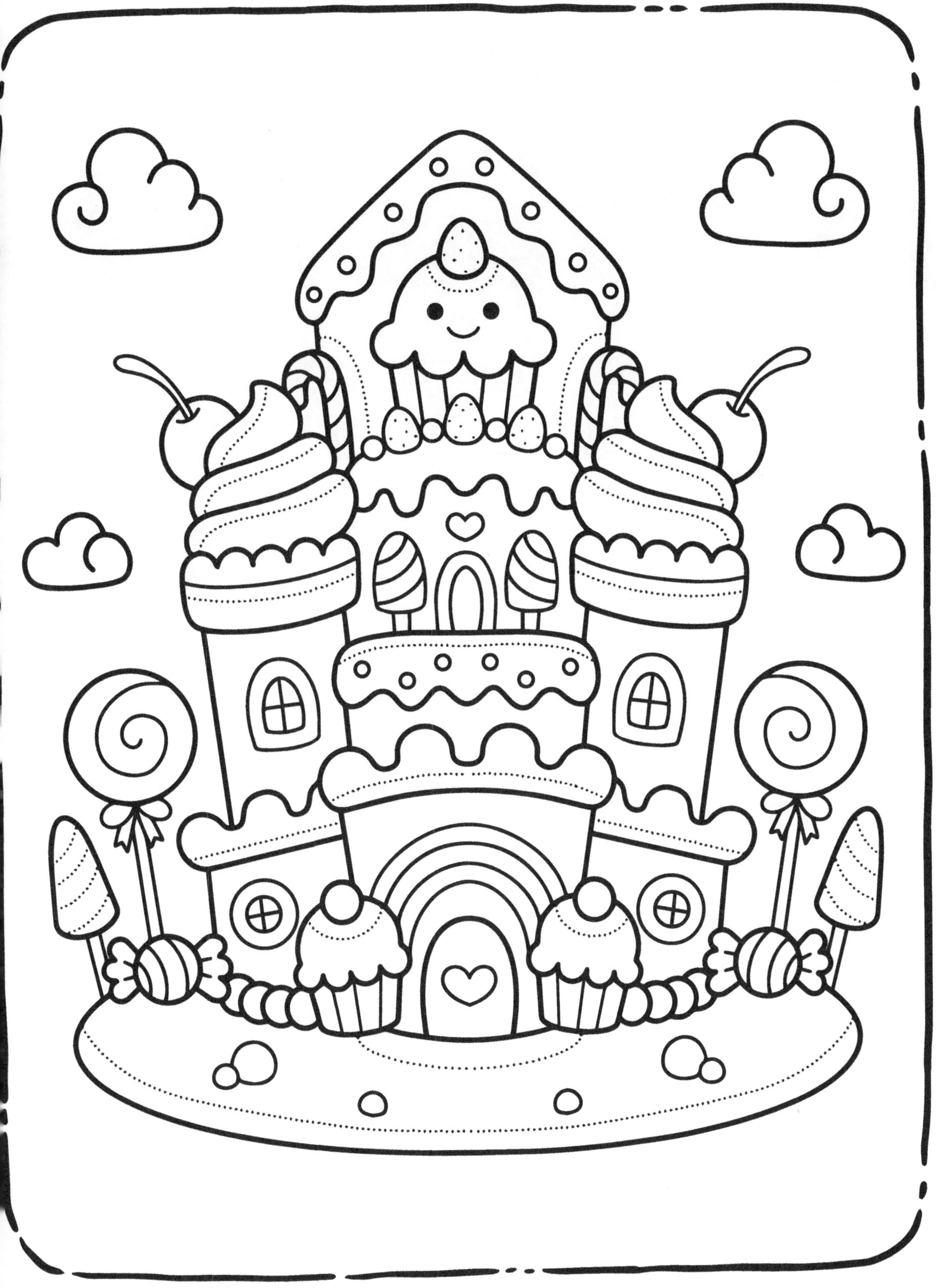

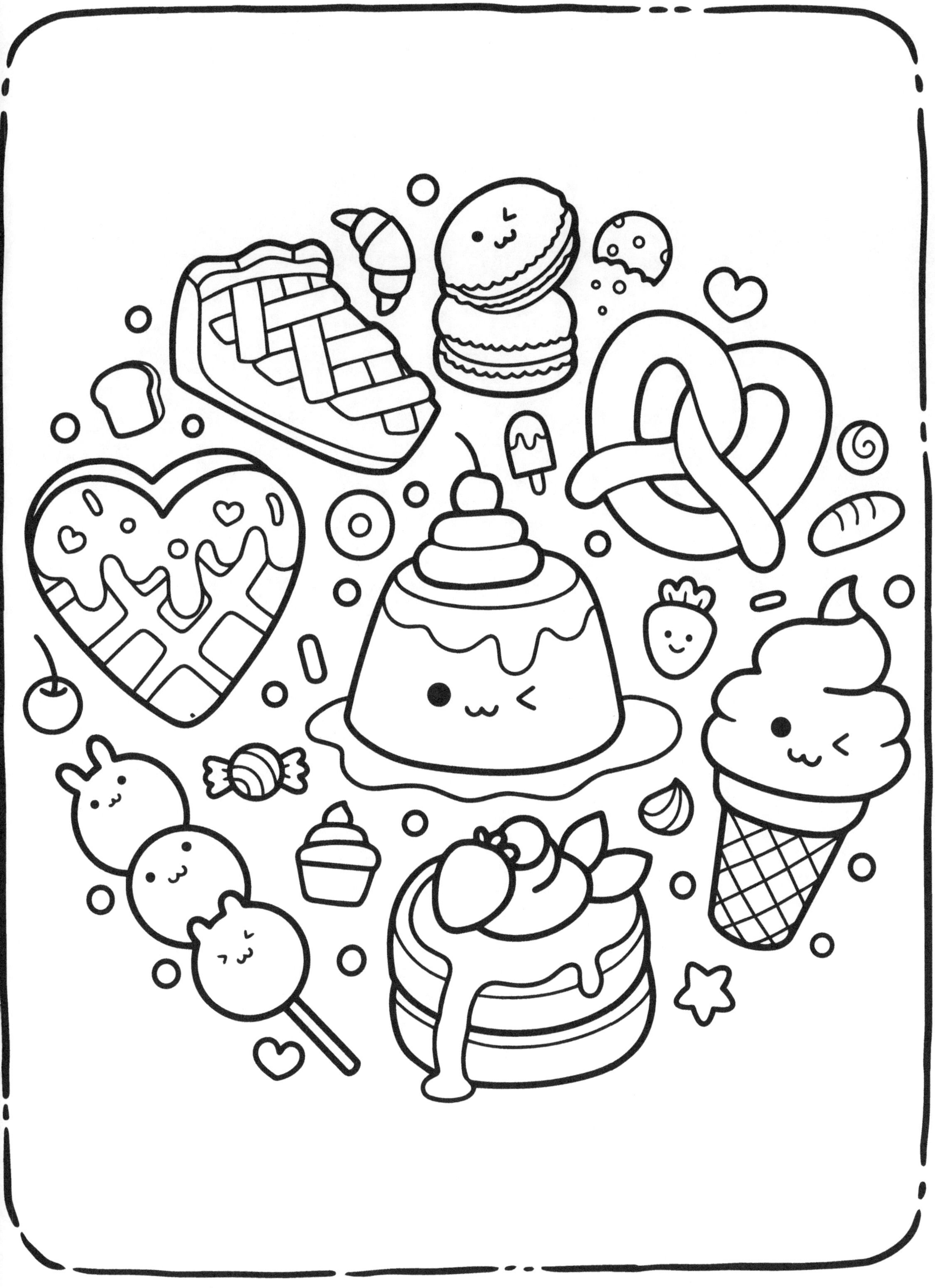

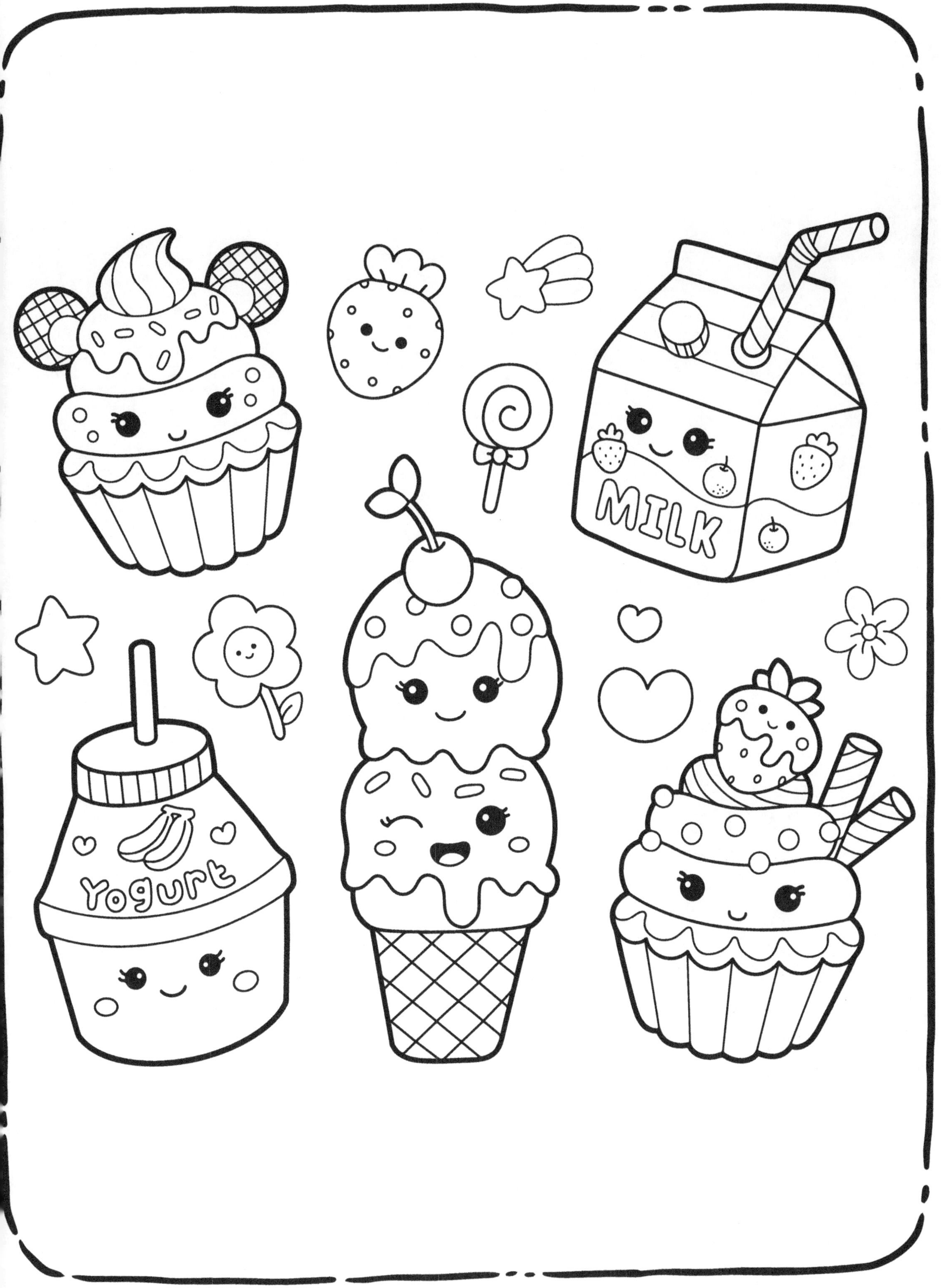
MILK
Yogurt

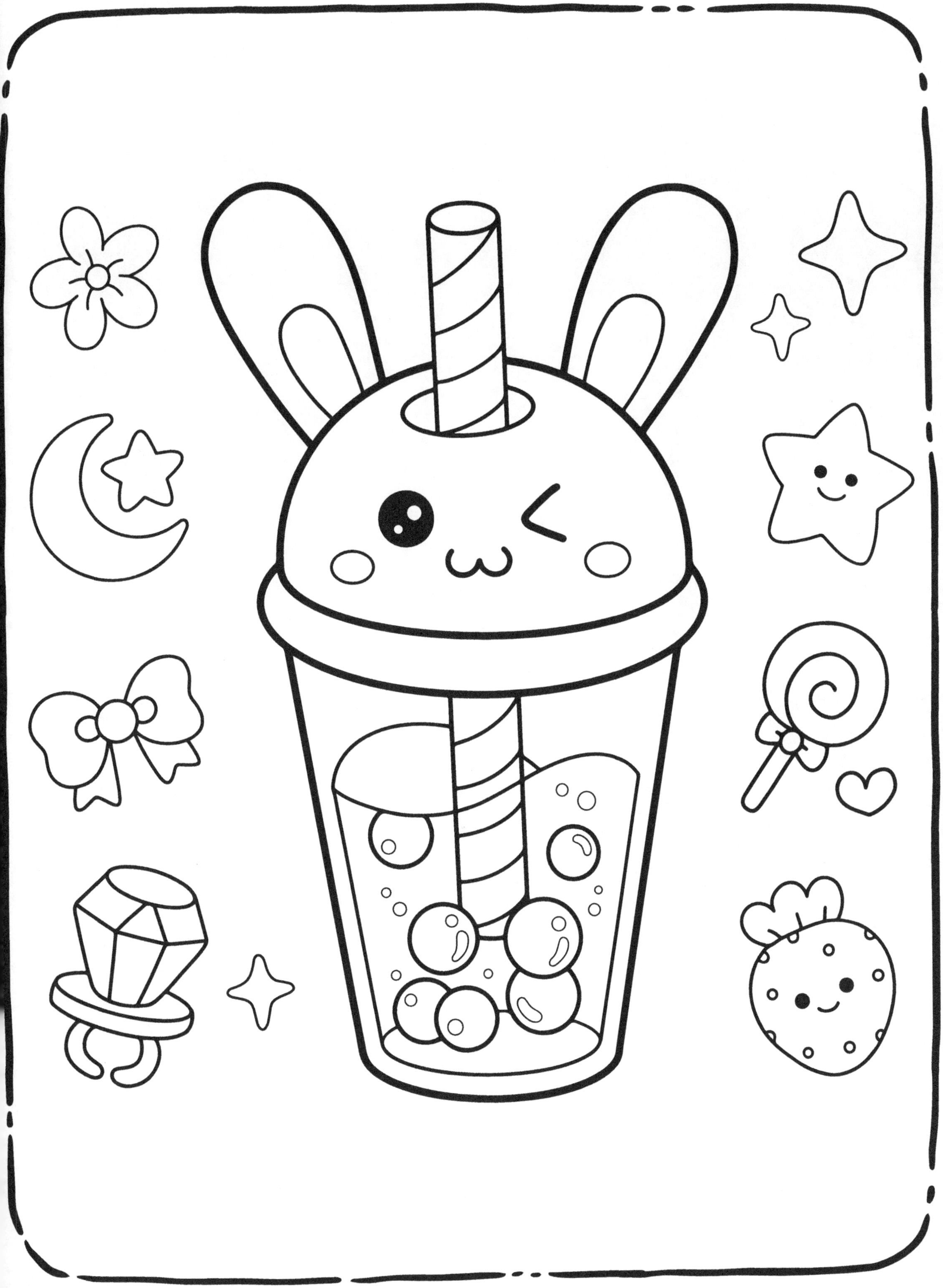

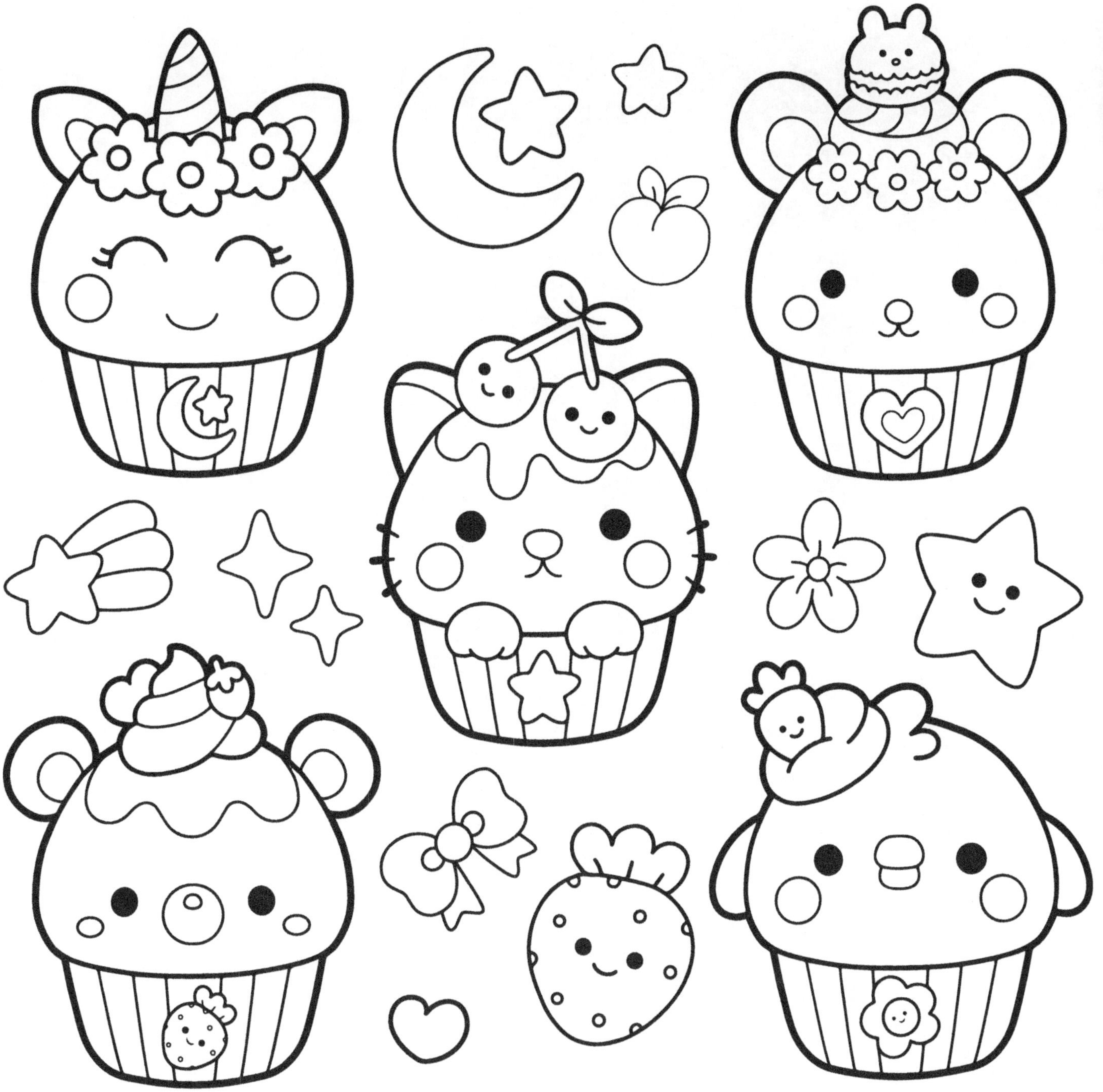

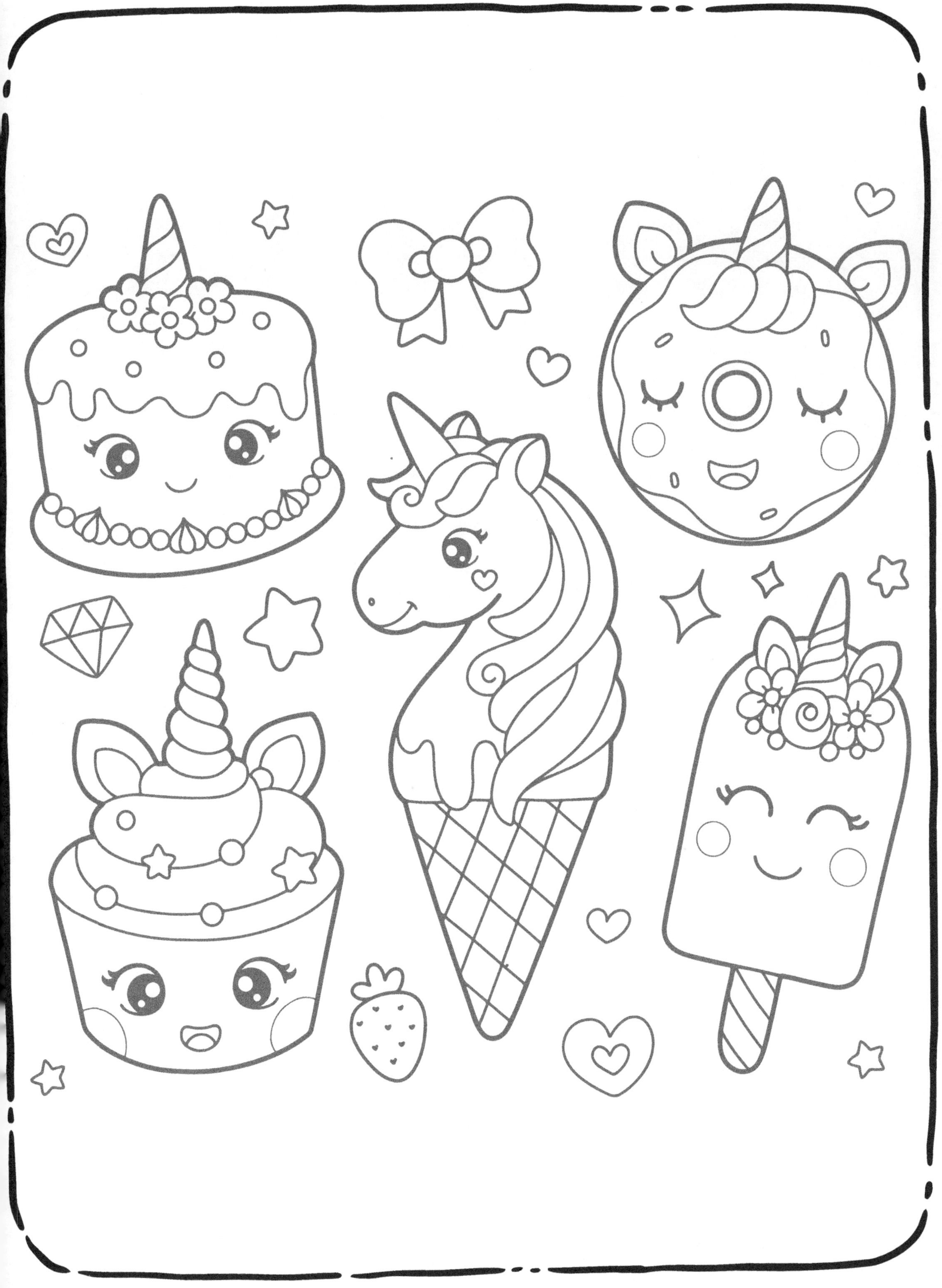

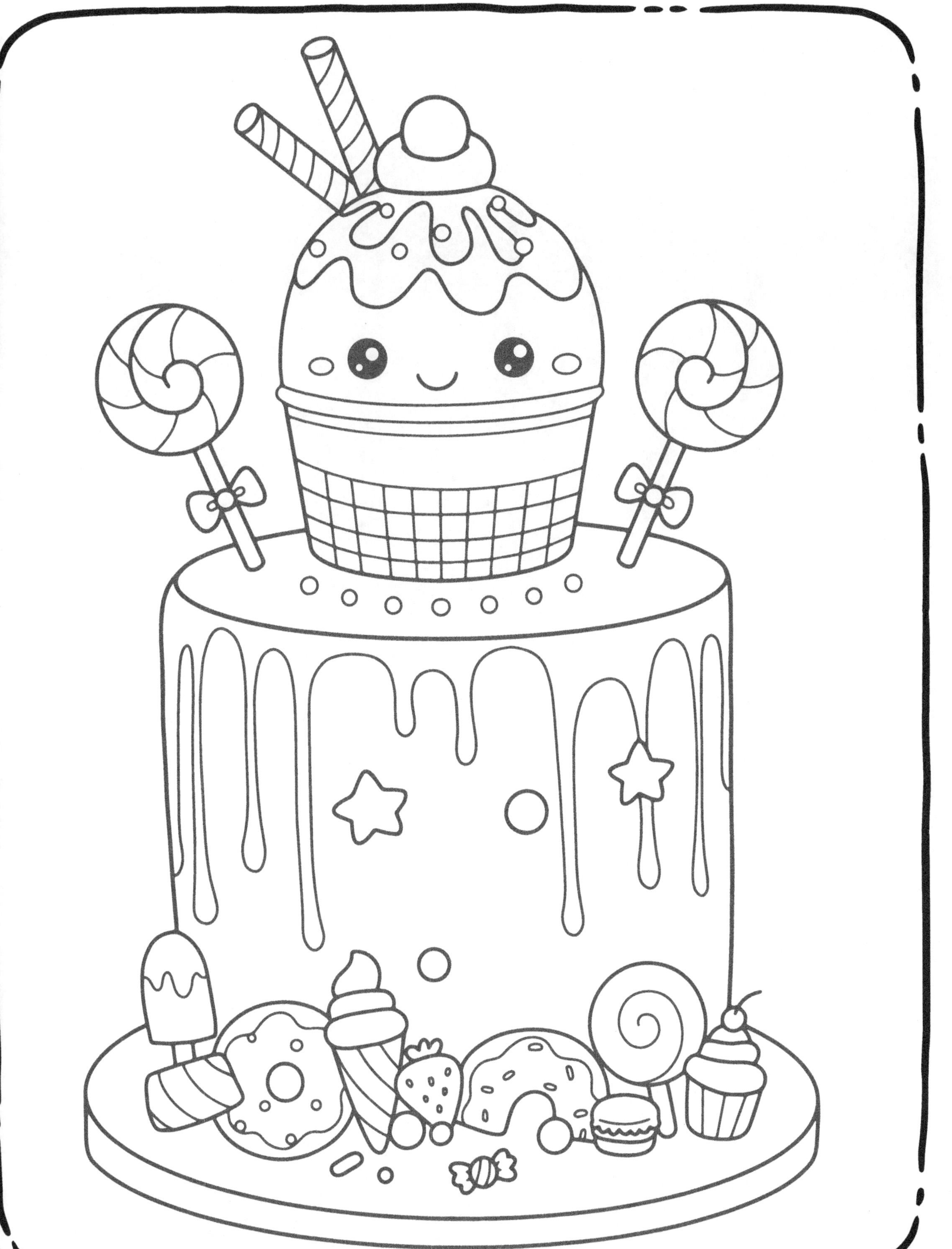

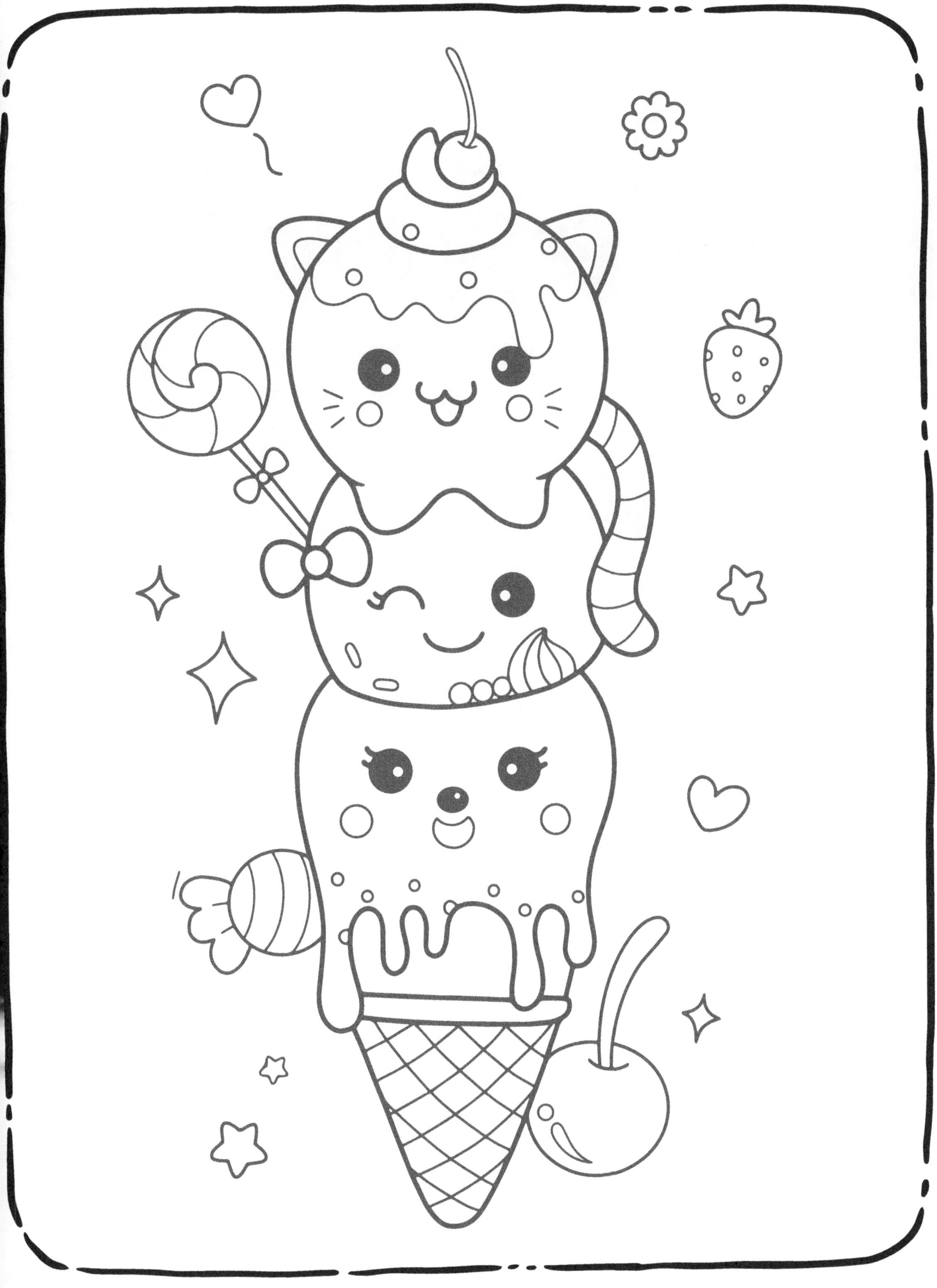

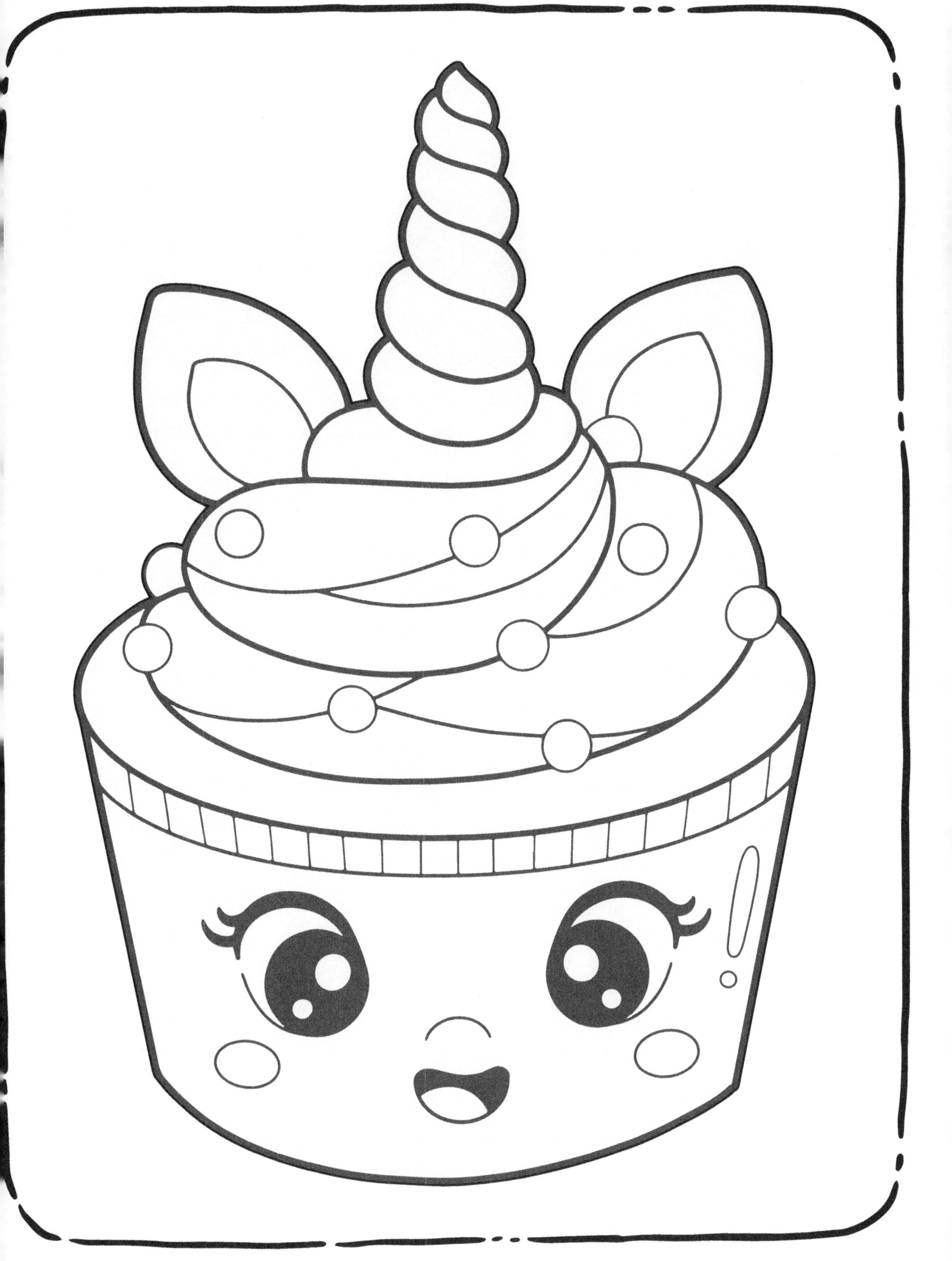

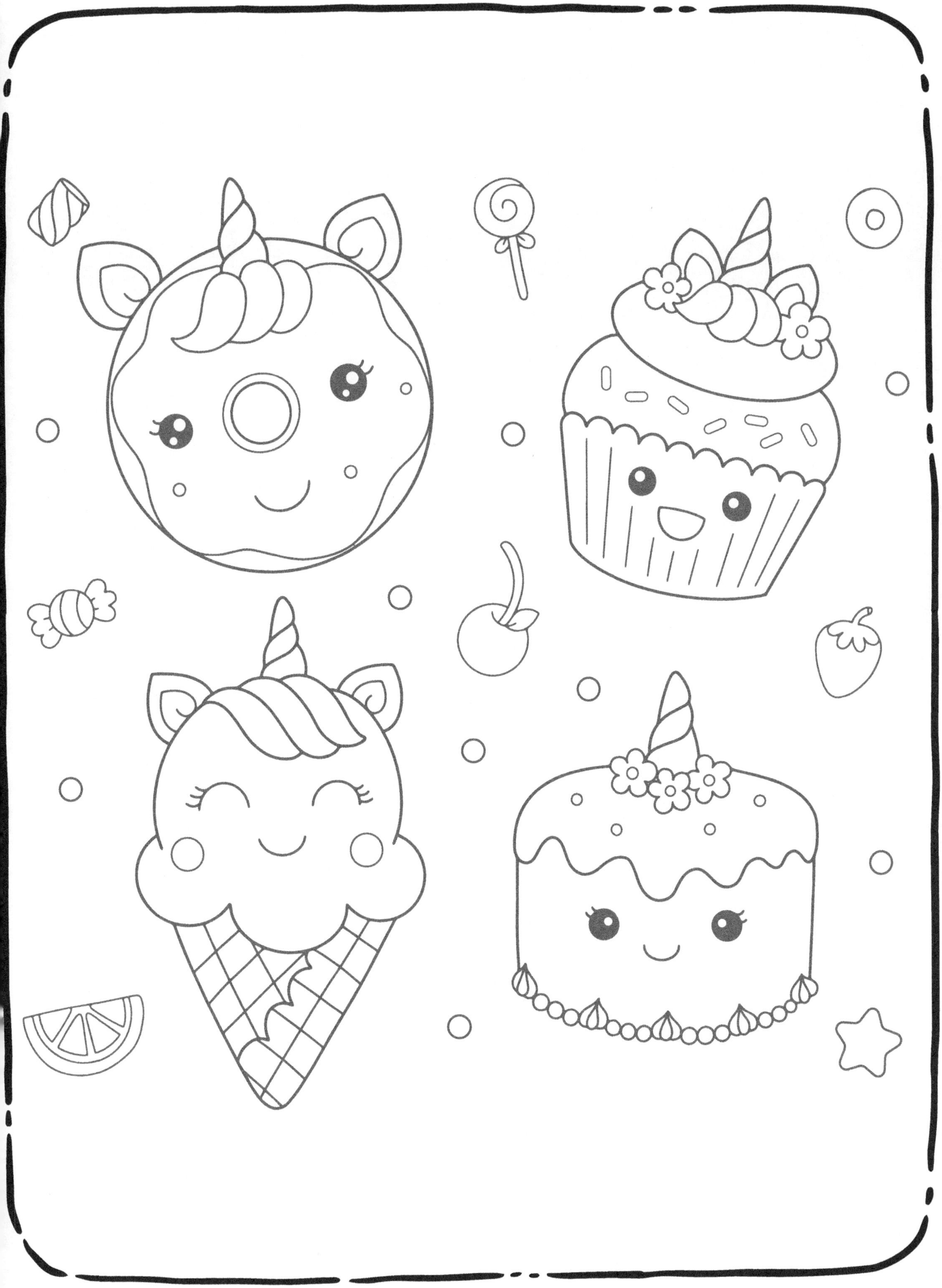

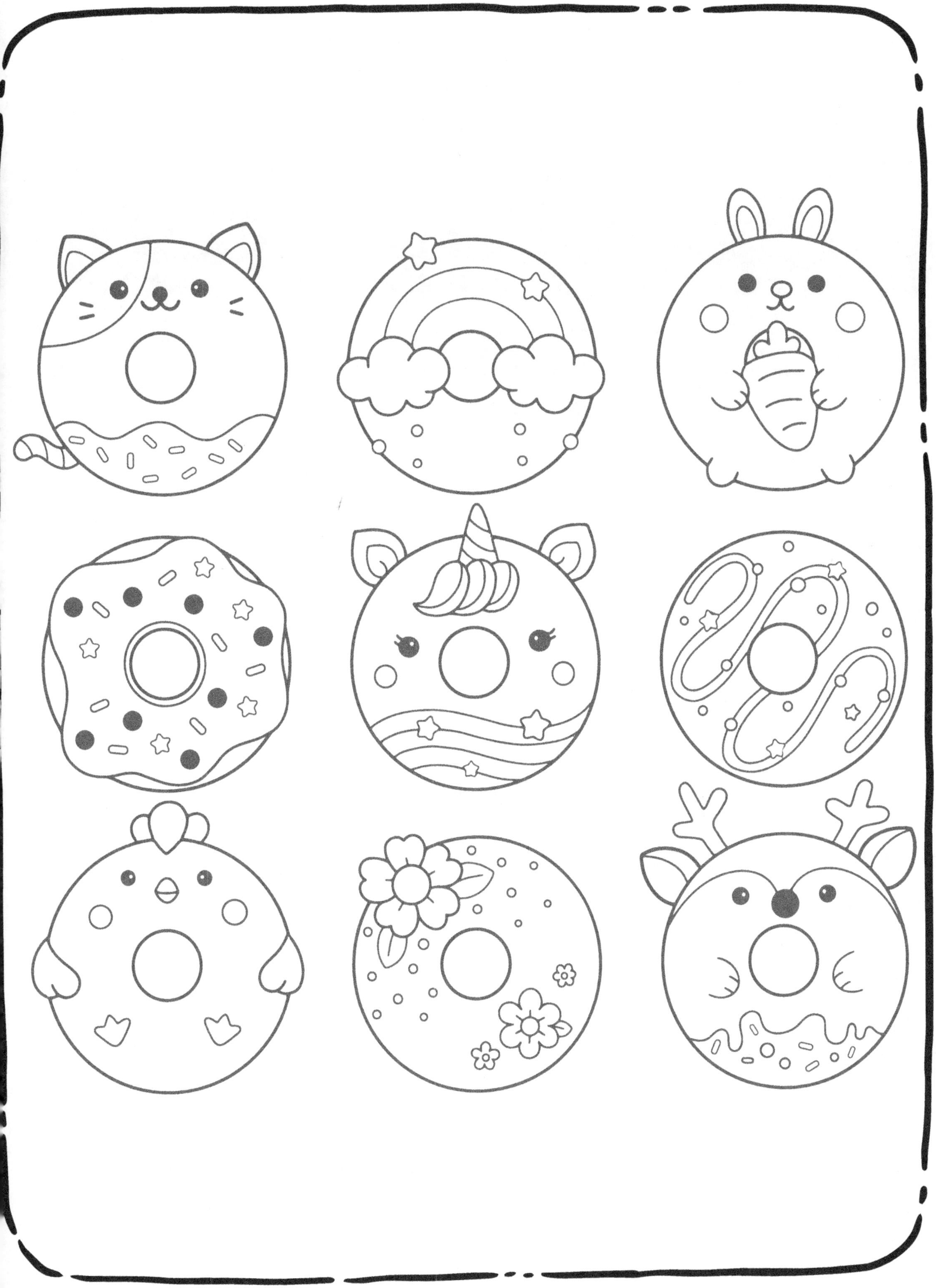

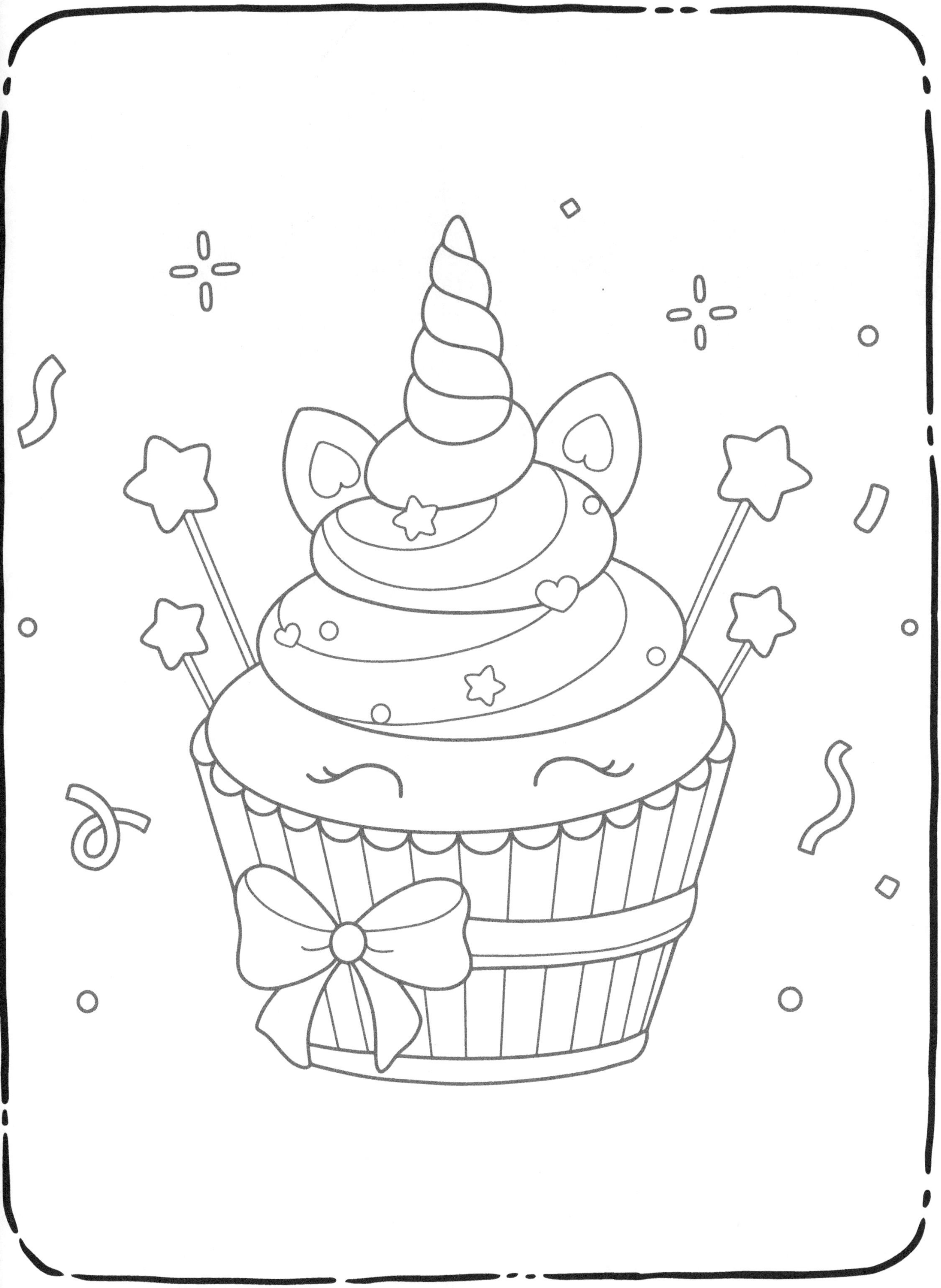

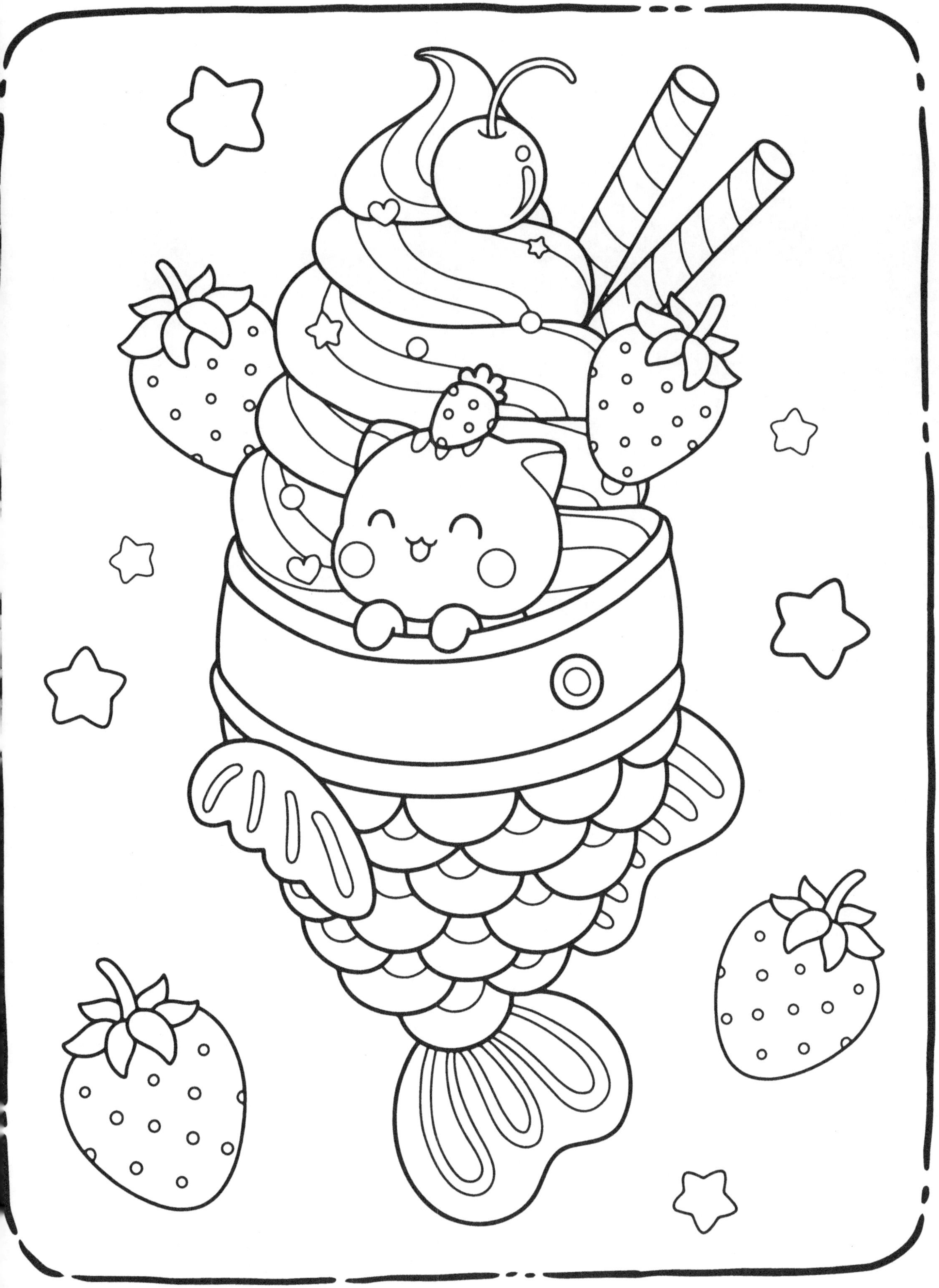

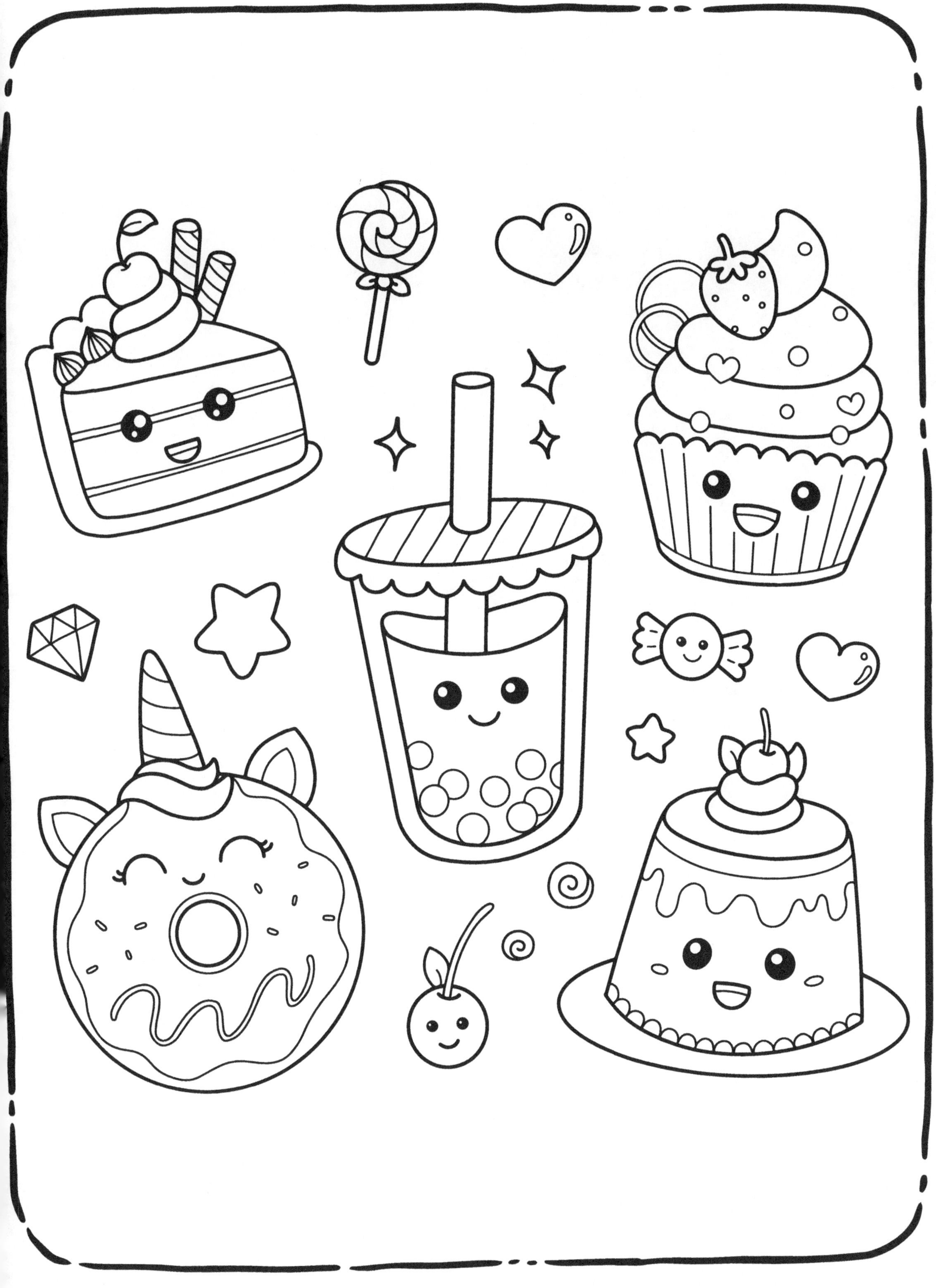

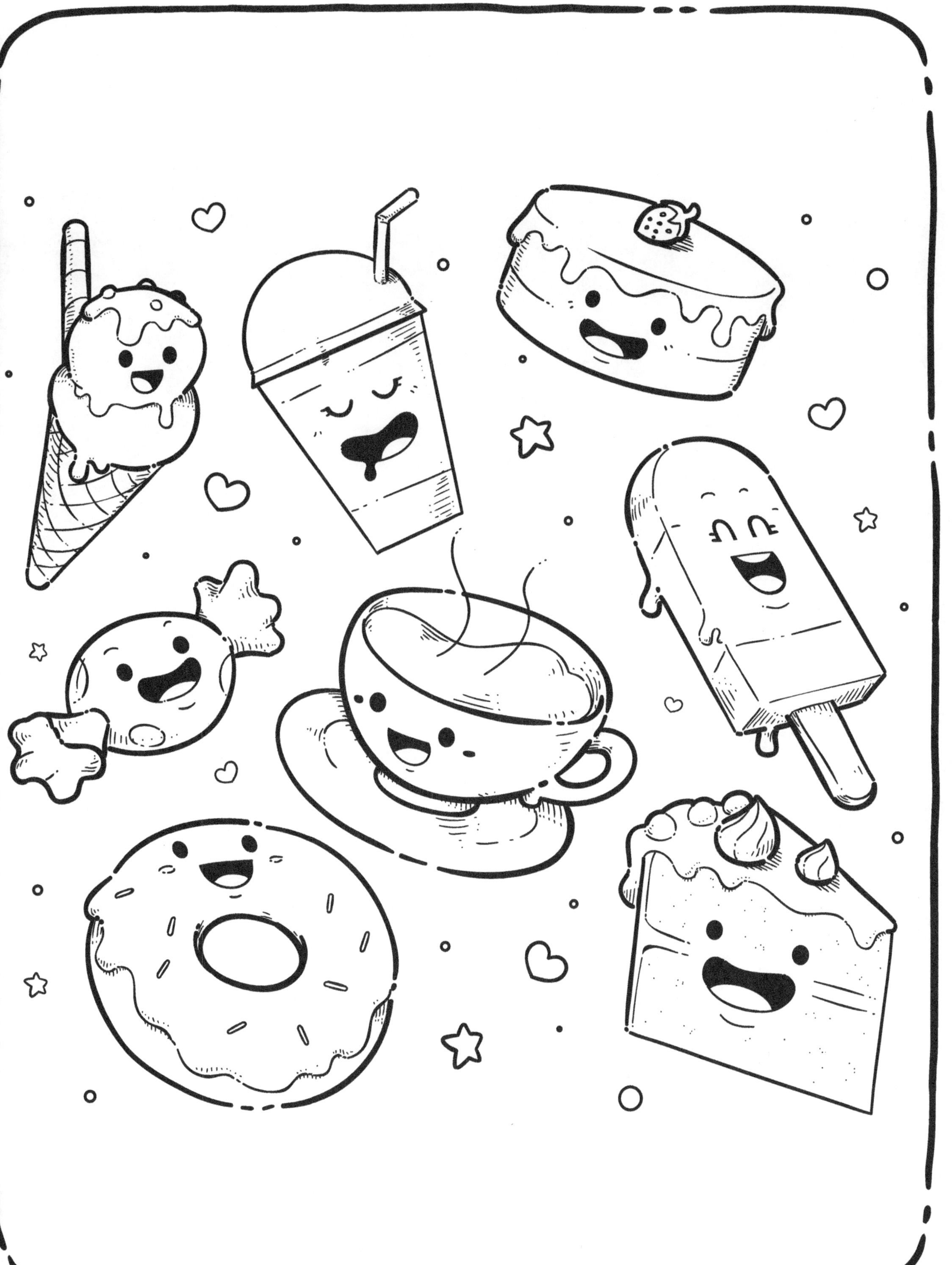

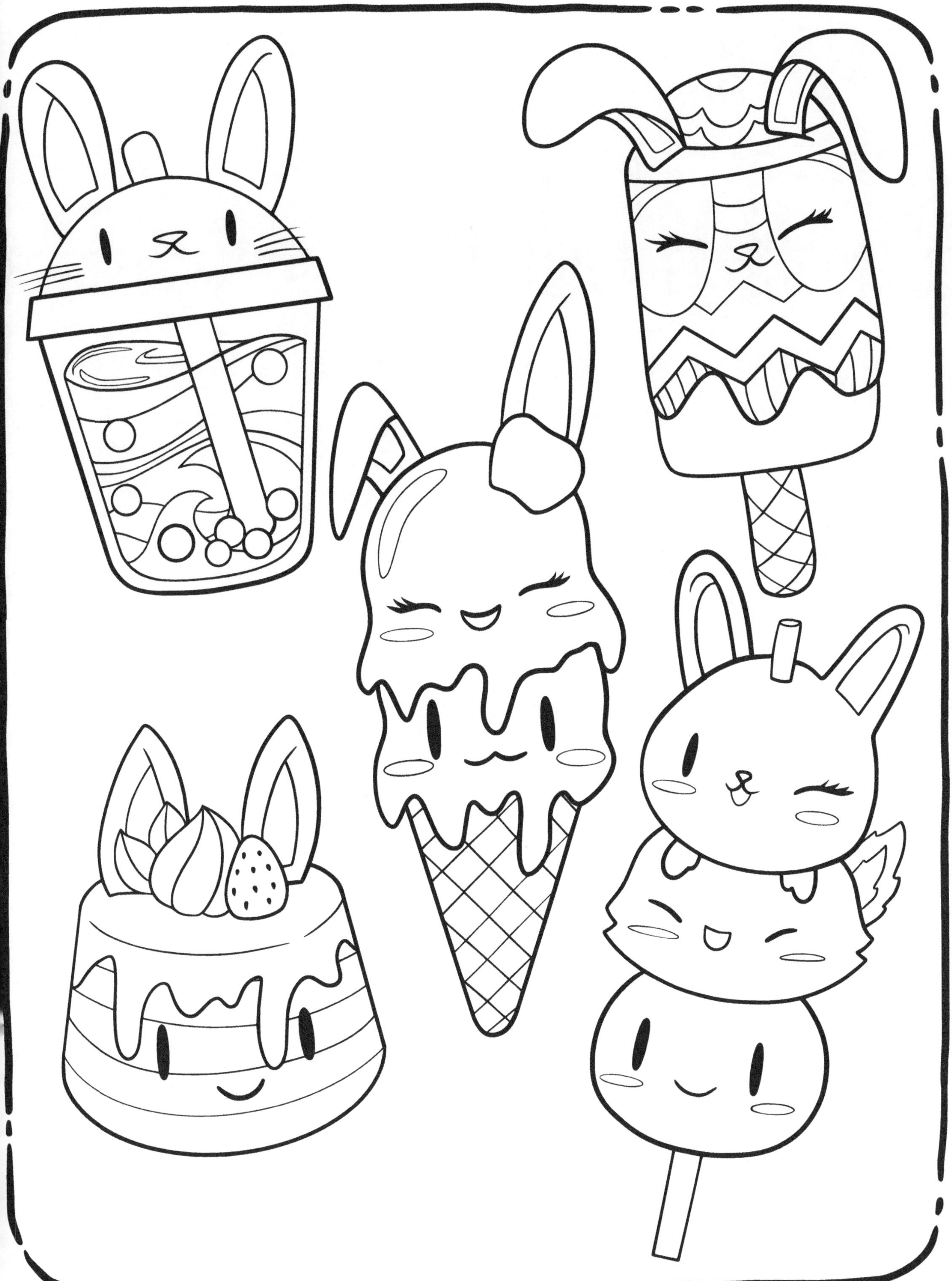

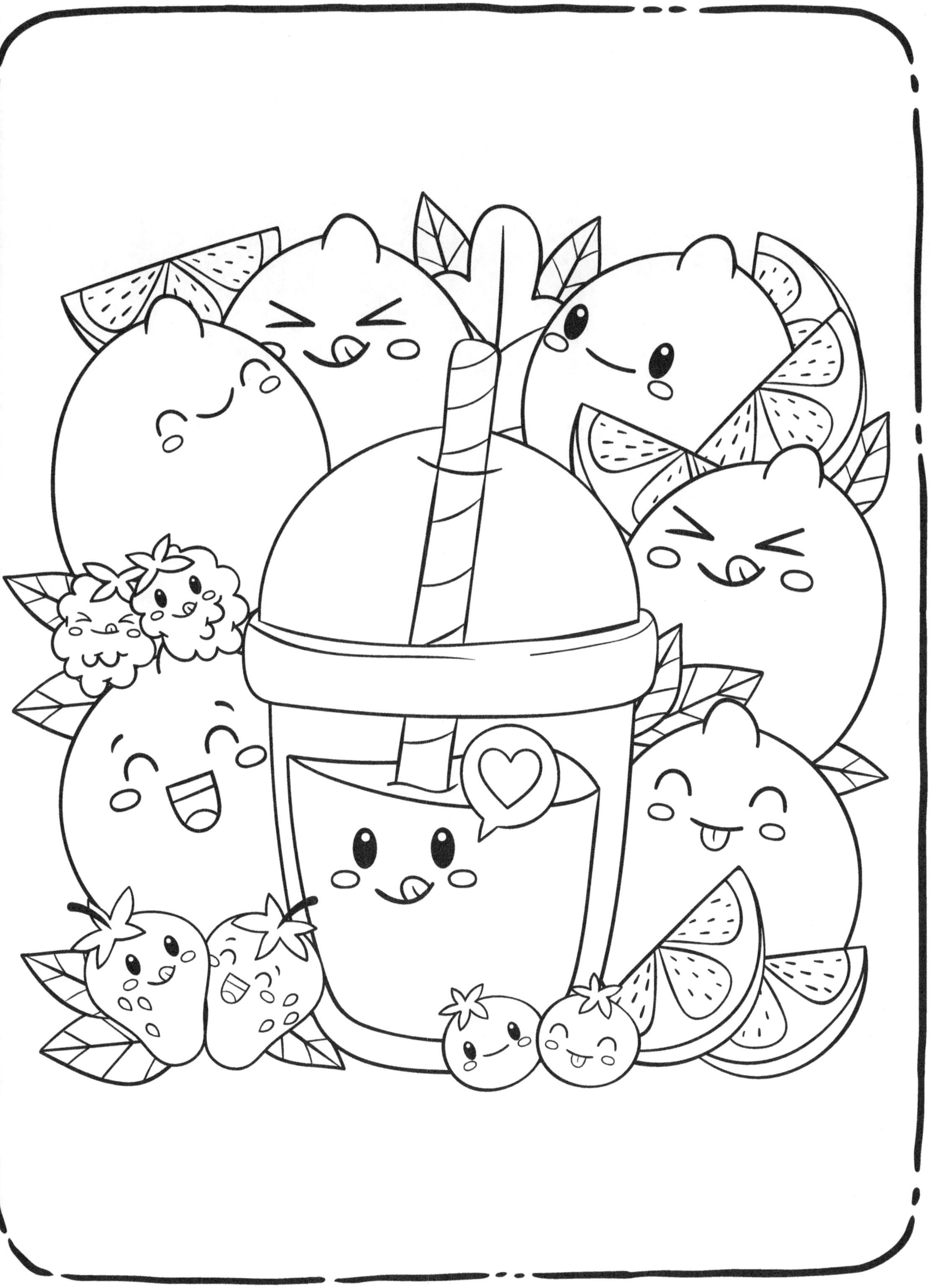

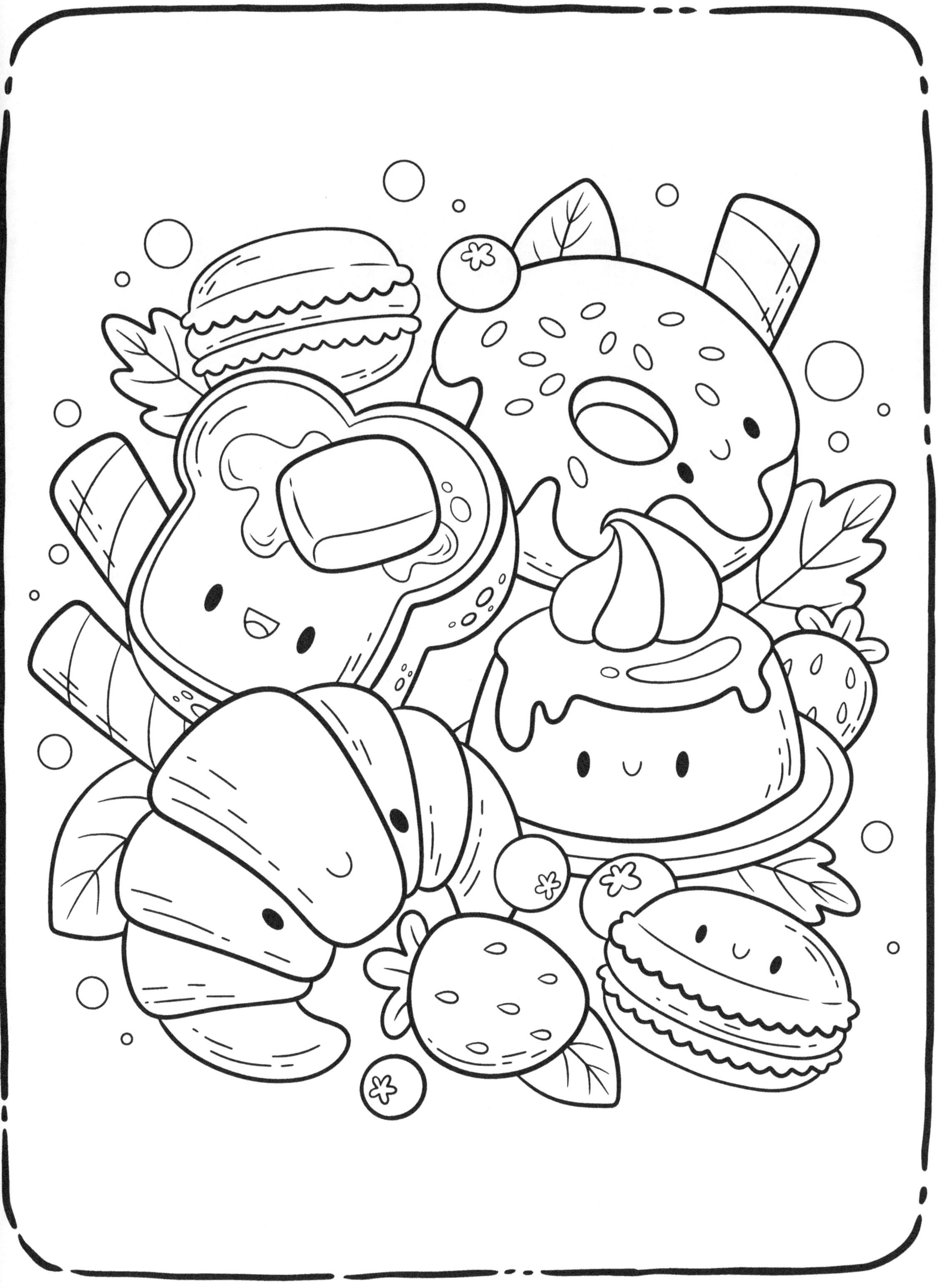

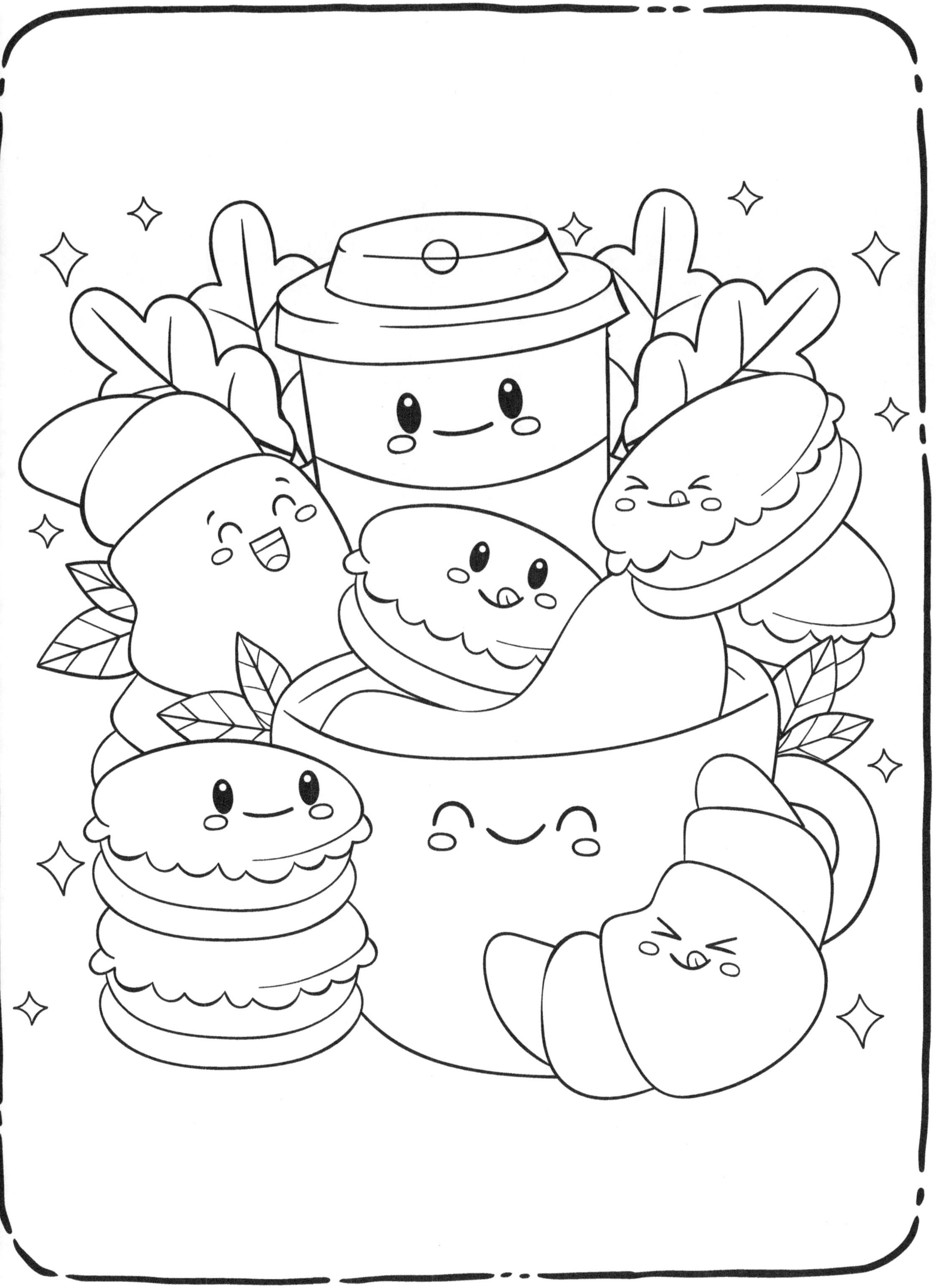

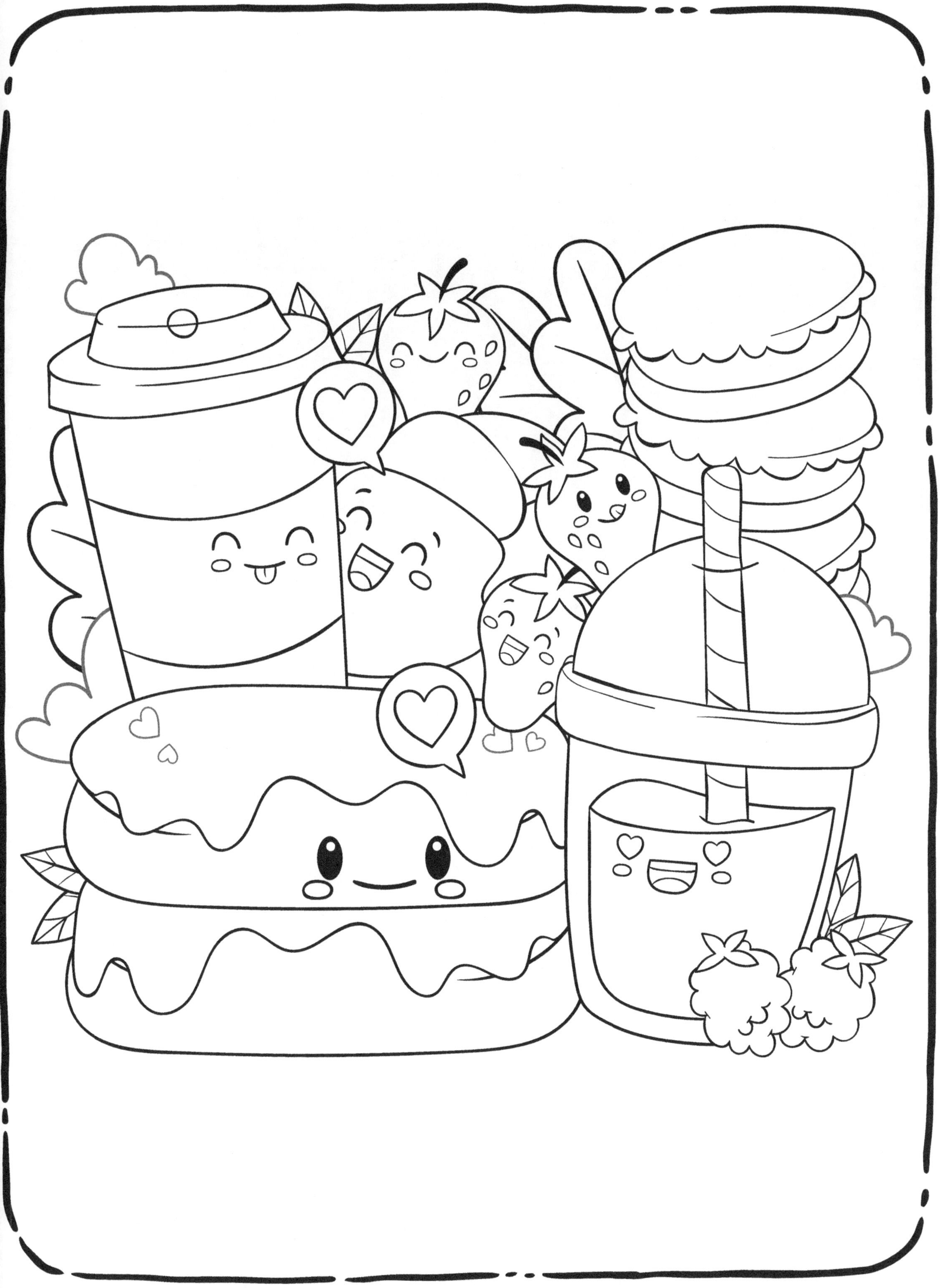

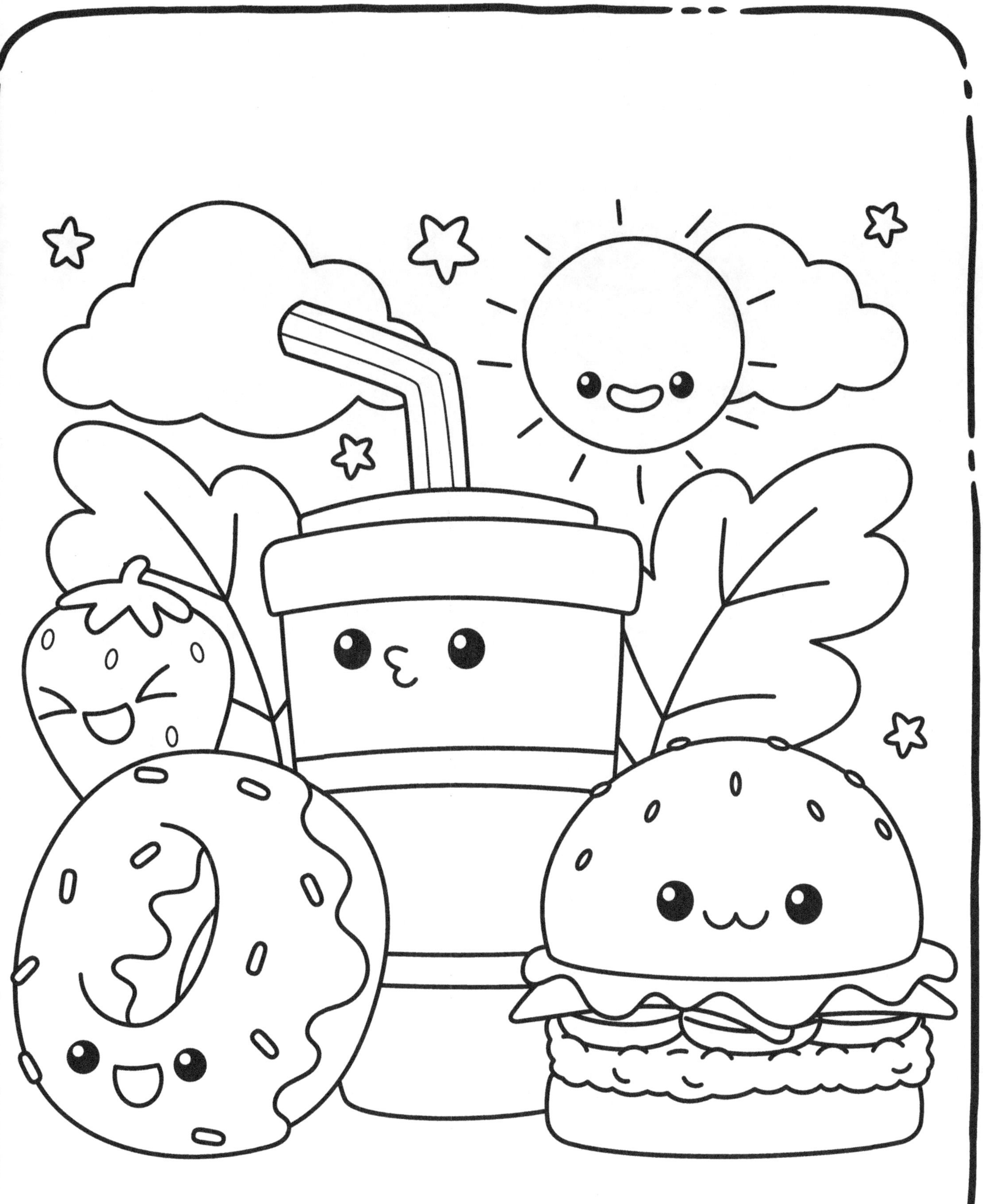

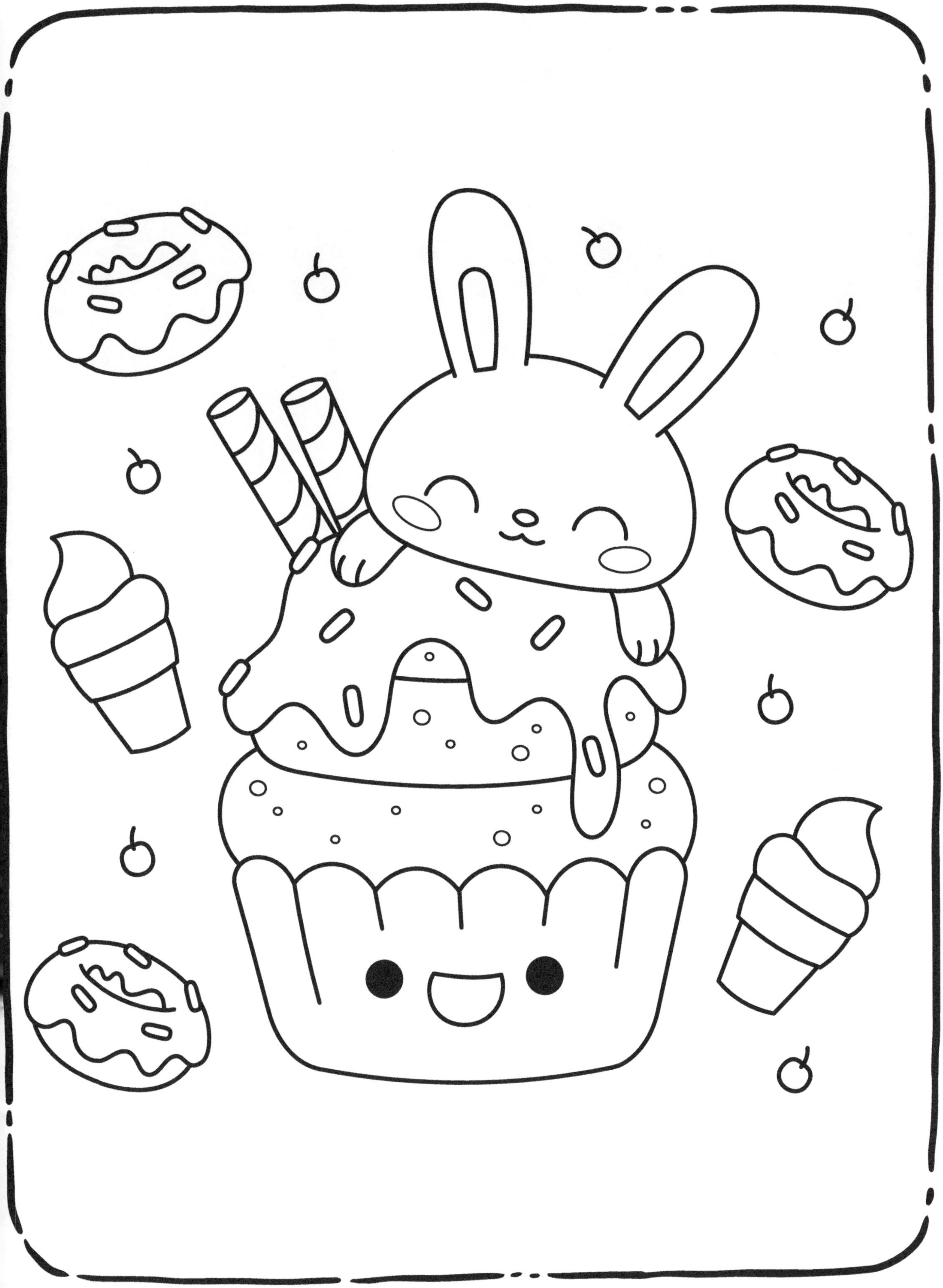

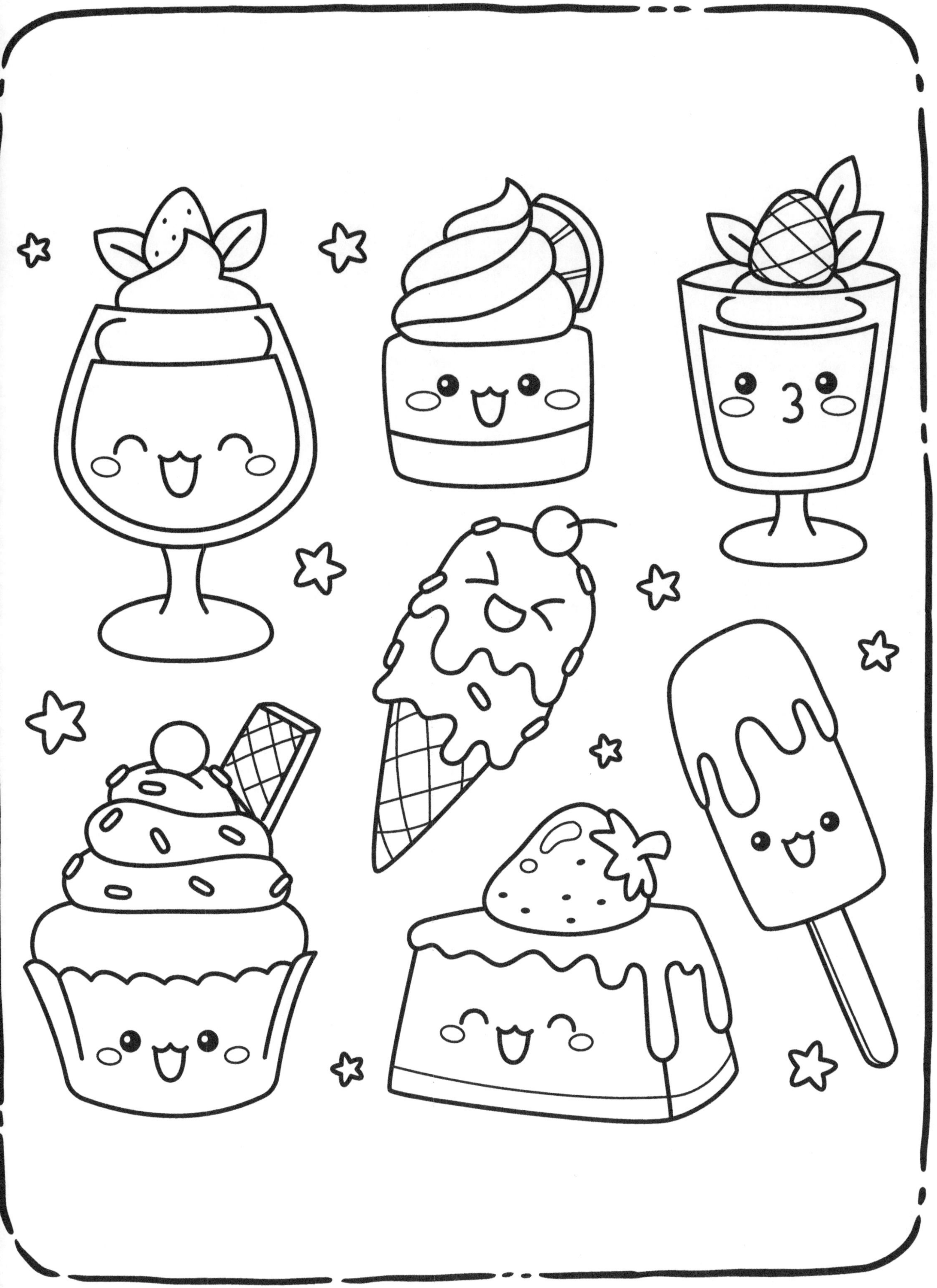

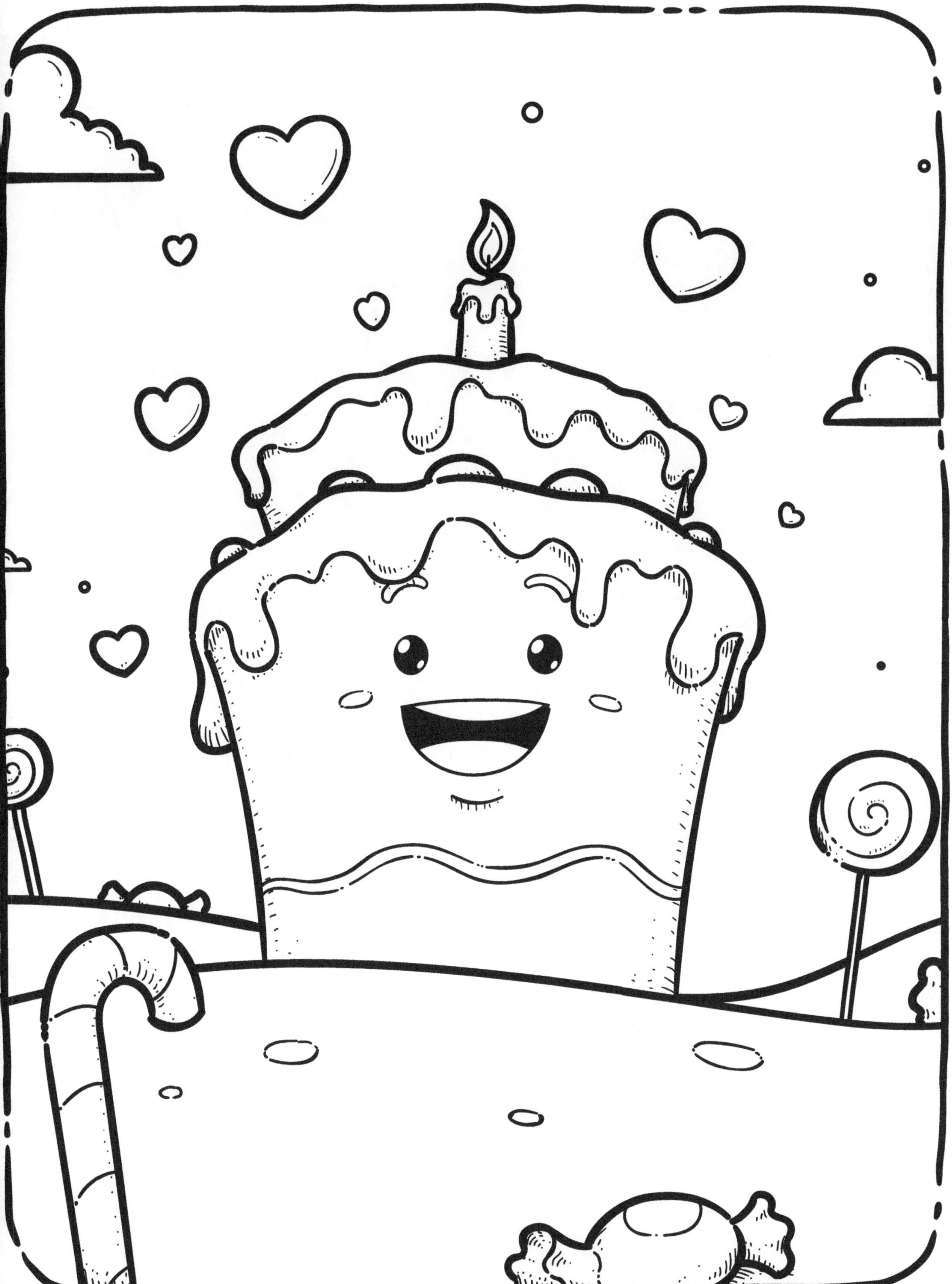

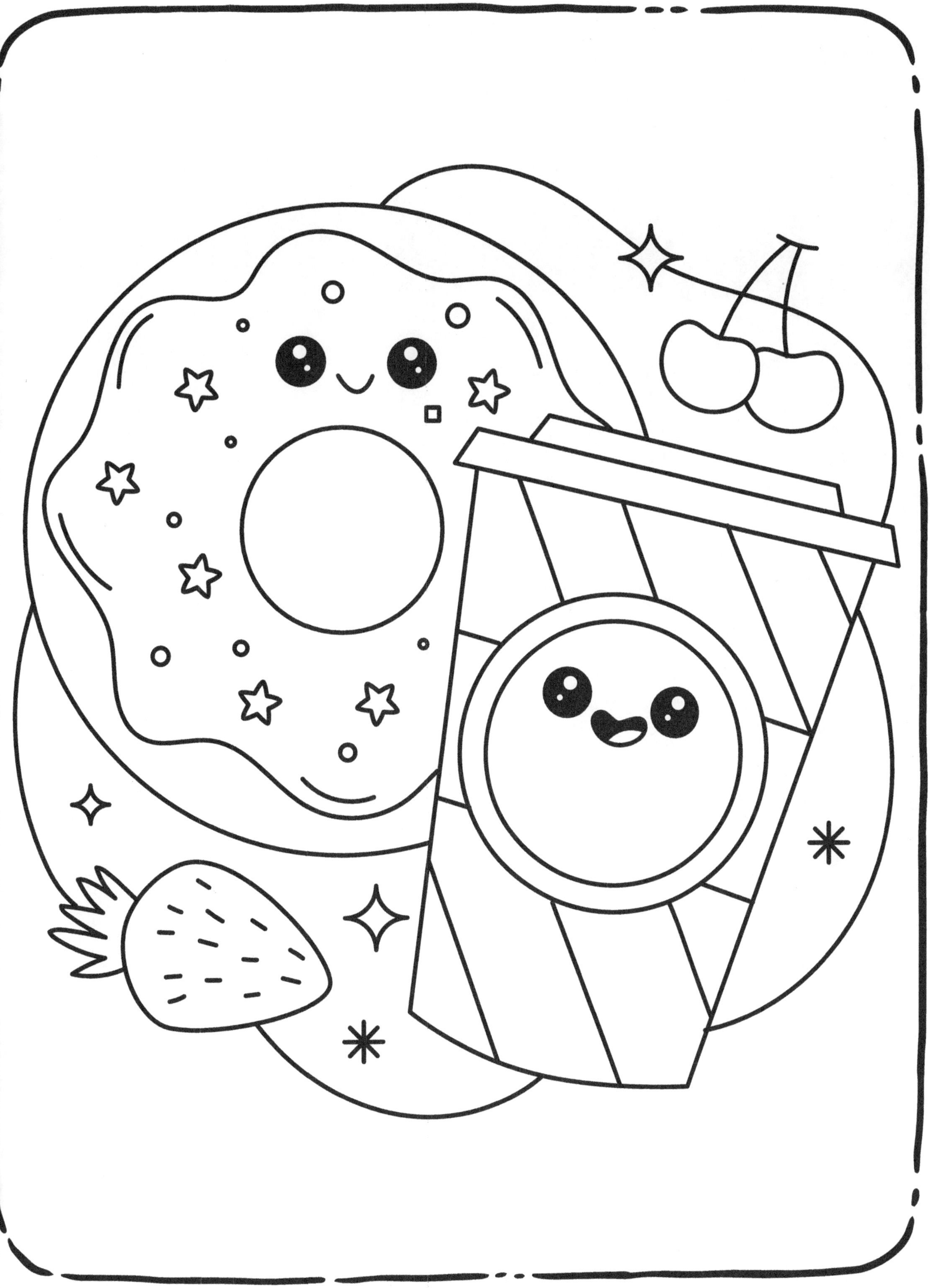

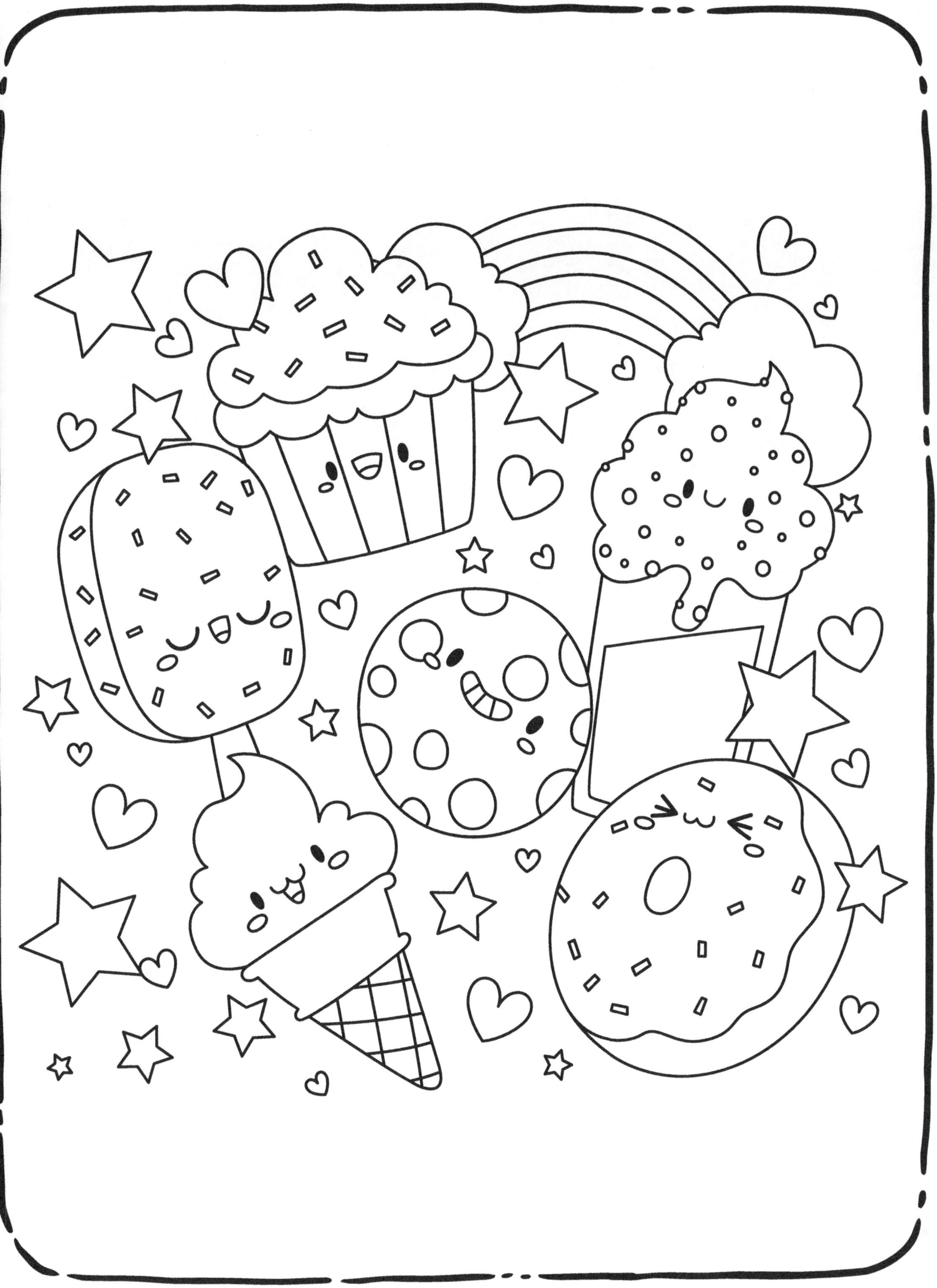

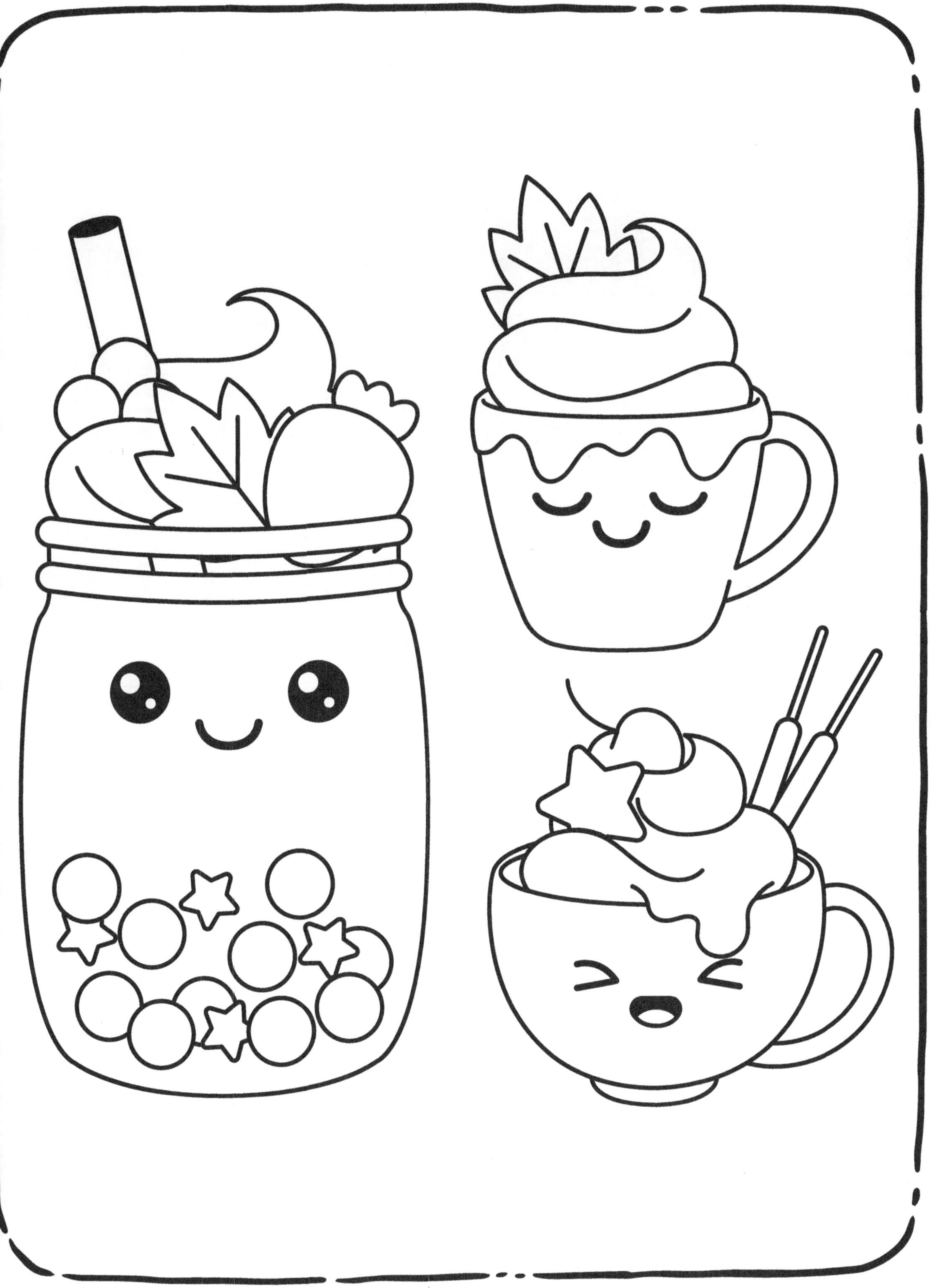

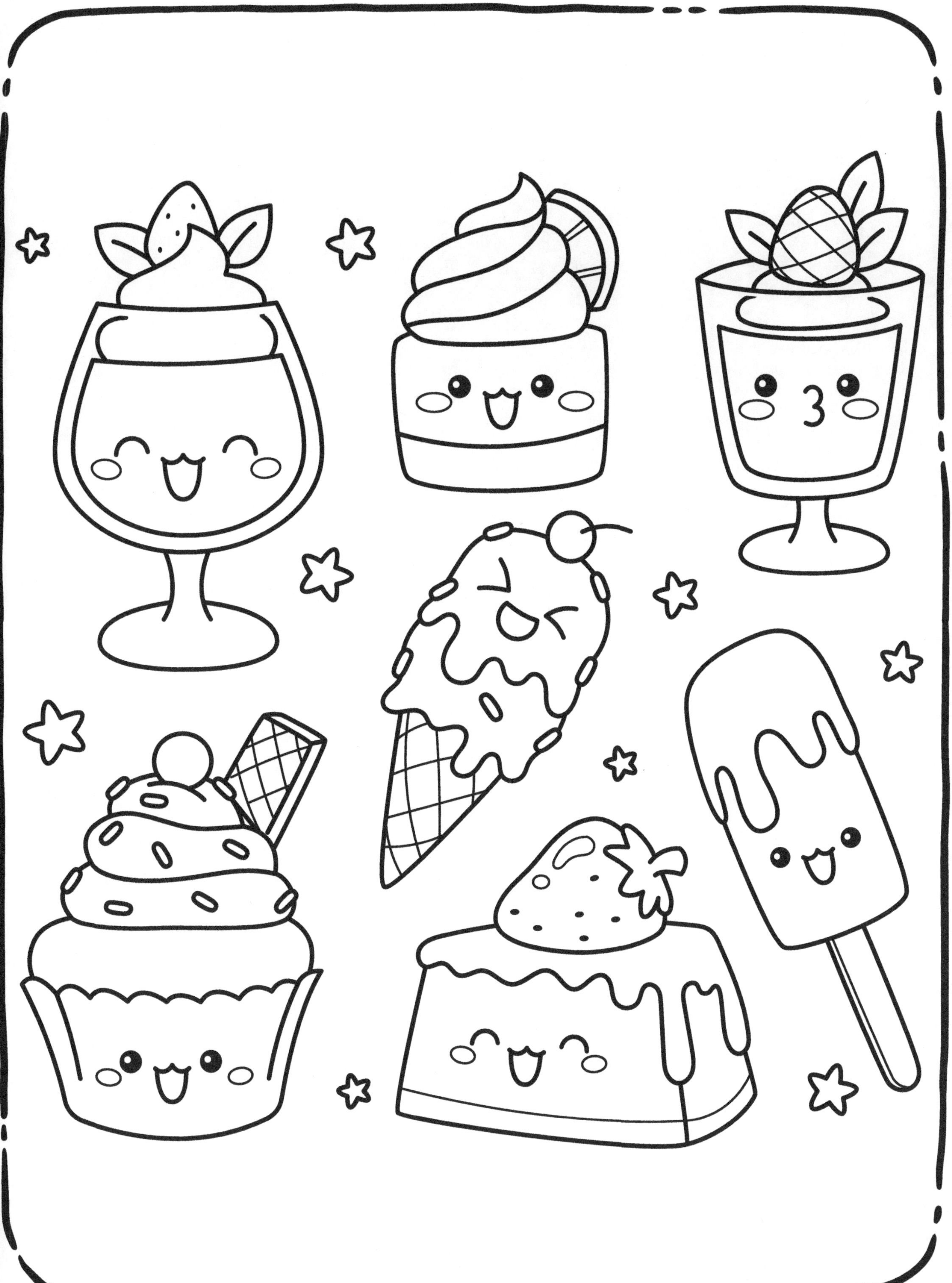

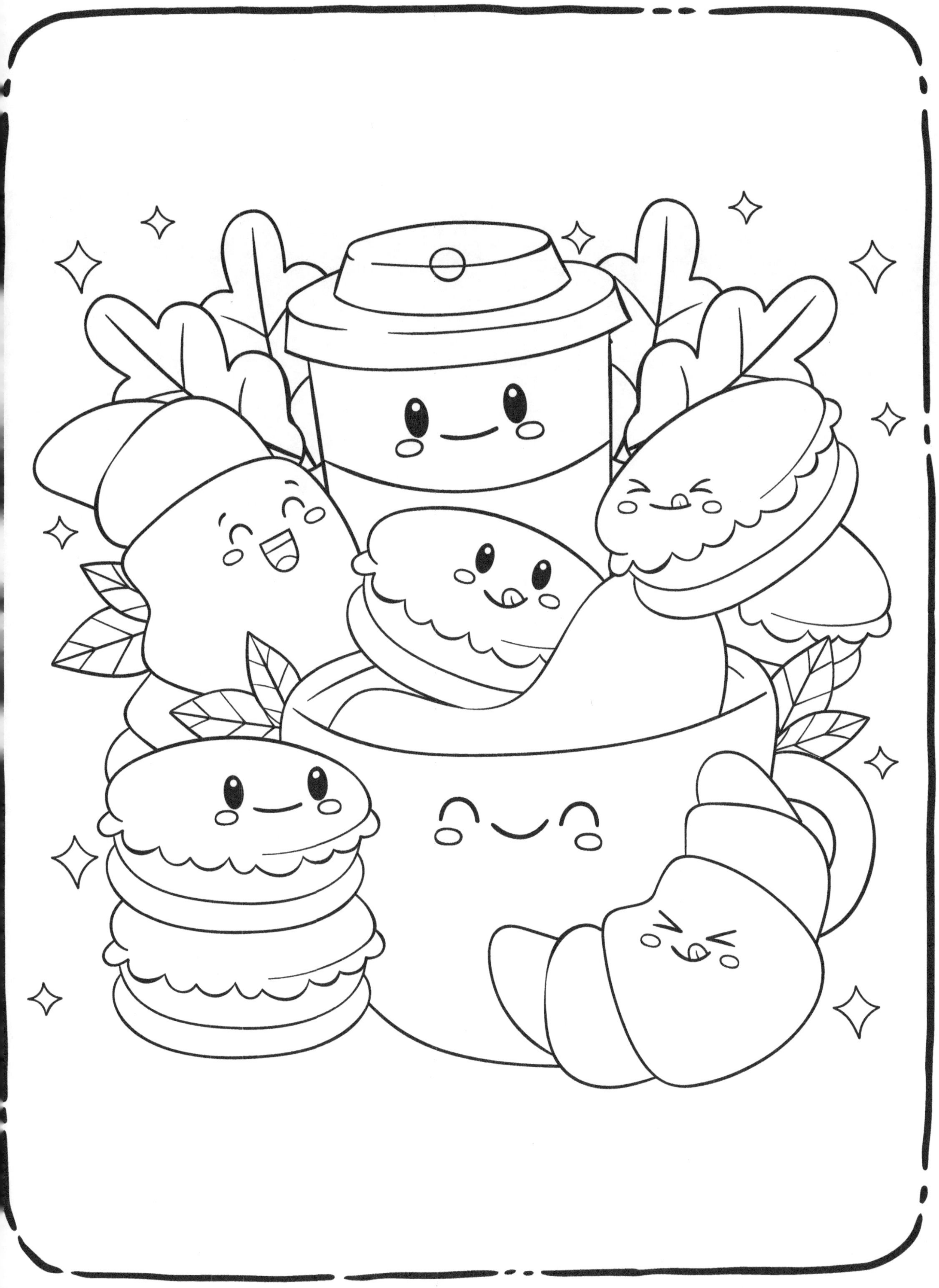

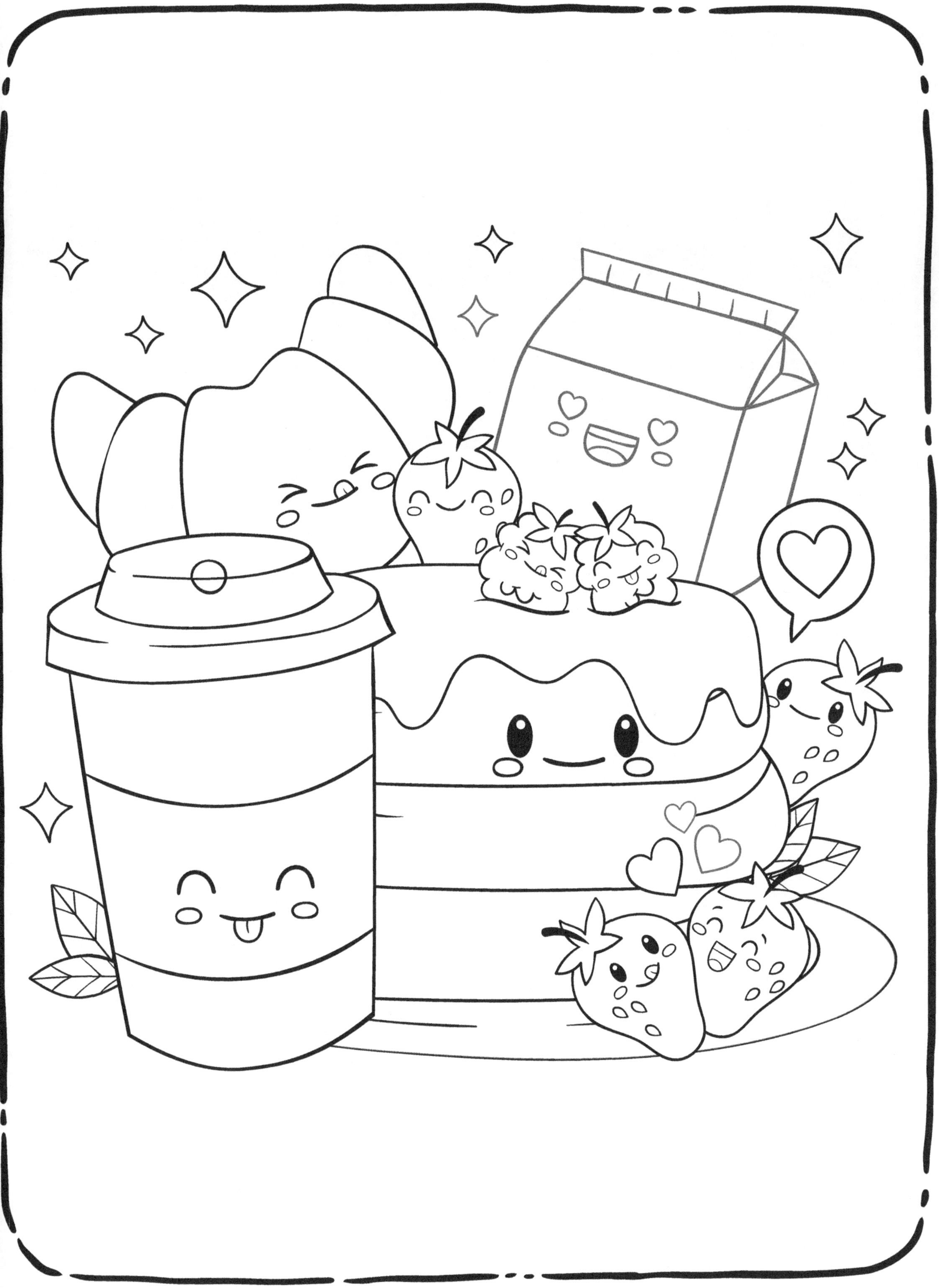

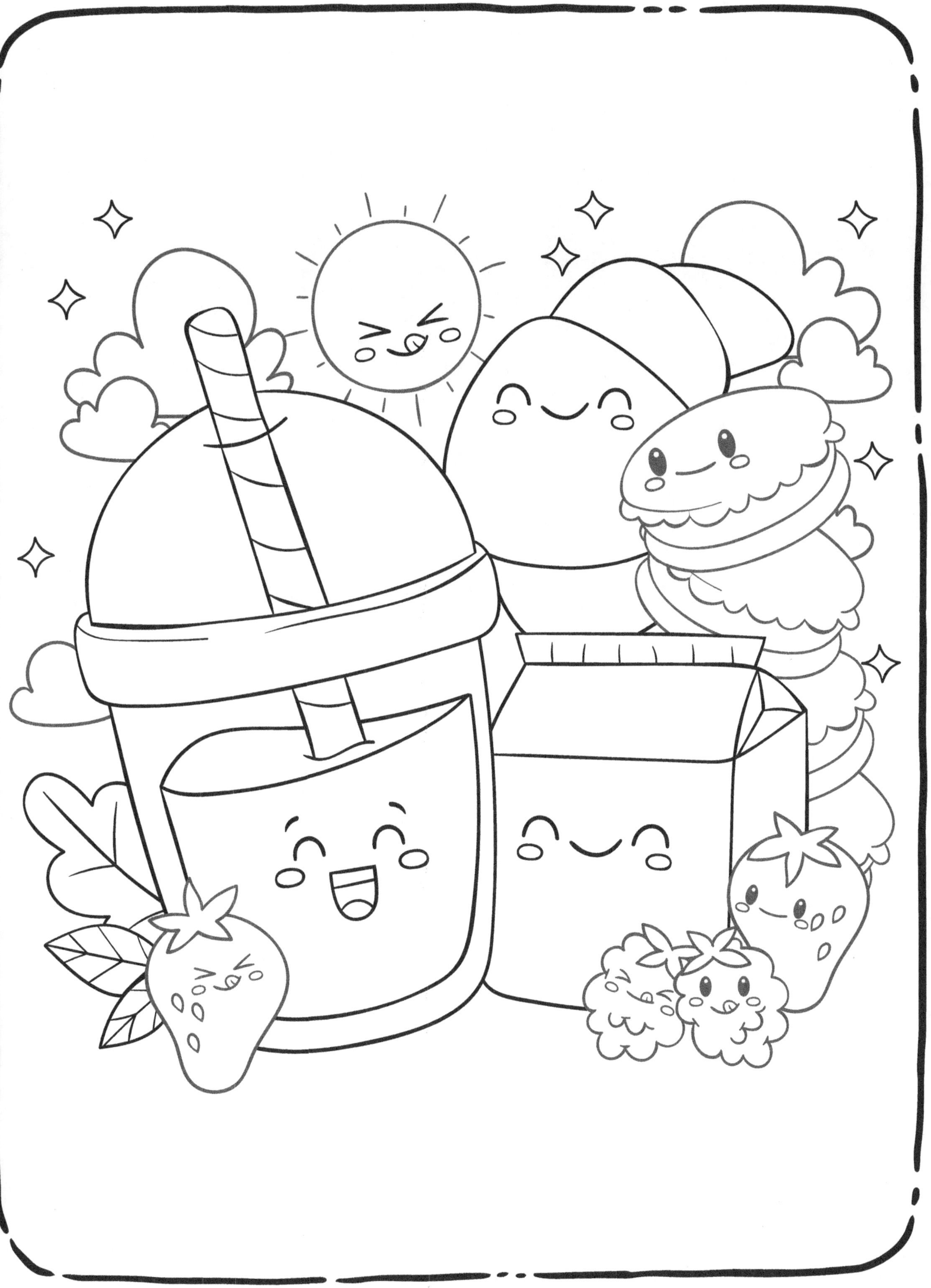

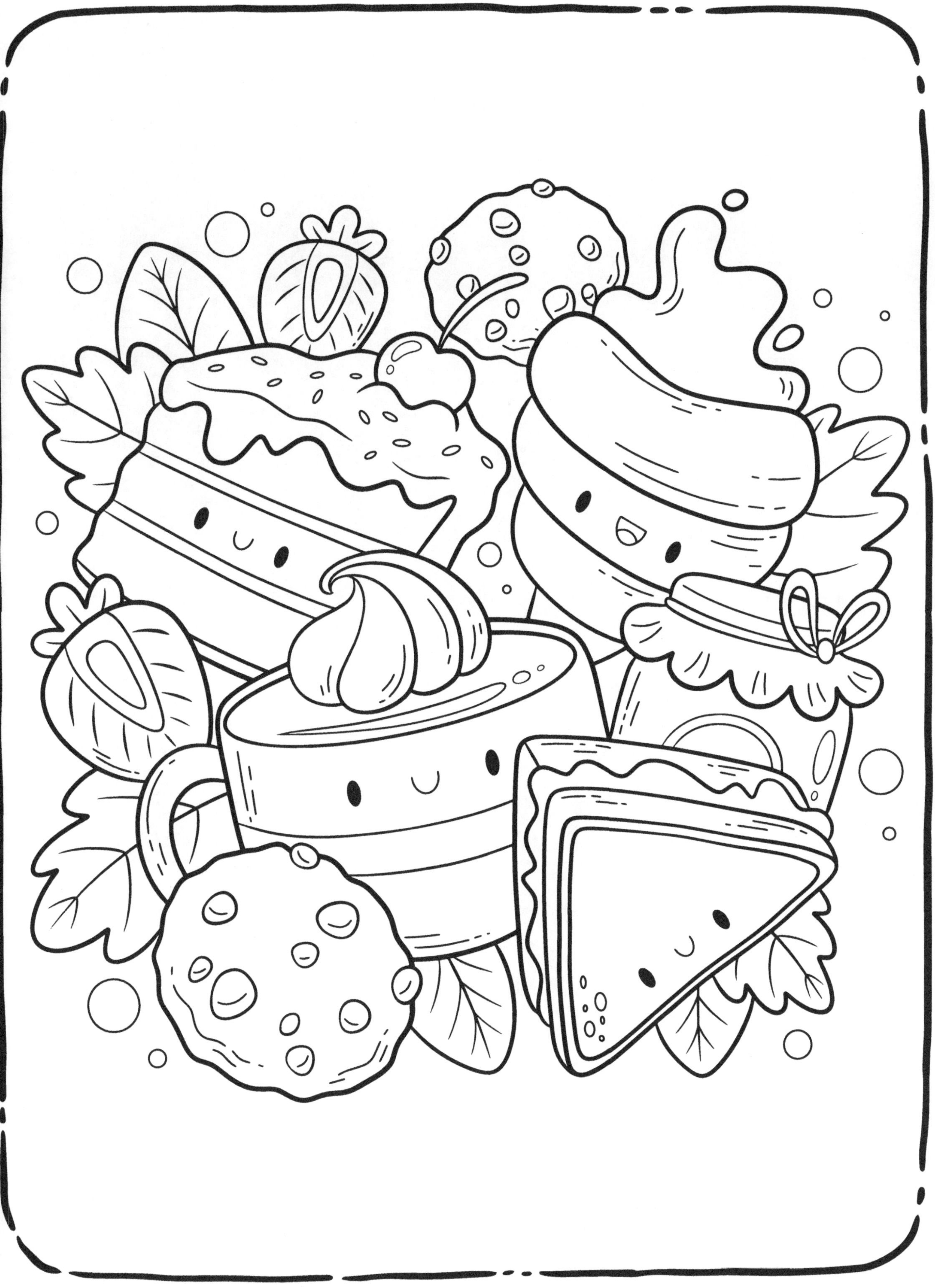

Made in the USA
Las Vegas, NV
20 November 2024

12164687R00044